AY PASTOR

Training Manual

Published by City Christian Publishing
9200 NE Fremont • Portland, Oregon 97220

Printed in the United States of America

City Christian Publishing is a ministry of City Bible Church and is dedicated to serving the local church and its leaders through the production and distribution of quality equipping resources. It is our prayer that these materials, proven in the context of the local church, will equip leaders in exalting the Lord and extending His kingdom.

For a free catalog of additional resources from City Christian Publishing, please call 1-800-777-6057 or visit our web site at *www.CityChristianPublishing.com*.

Lay Pastor Training Manual – Student Edition
© Copyright 1997 by Frank Damazio
ISBN 1-886849-06-4

Lay Pastor Training

Foreword

Our church has experienced steady growth, spiritually and numerically, for four decades. We have made changes or course adjustments as were necessary to accomplish the vision set before us. This new addition enhances our broad scope of ministry involvement. Lay pastors enable us not only to reap the harvest but to keep the harvest through more strategic discipling and nurturing. We have been able to spread the work load from the eldership to our lay pastors through this exciting, new structure. Through lay pastors we have developed manageable spans of care, enabling leaders to provide effective care. Our strategy is to continue to provide a ministry structure that pastors the whole church, reaching both those who participate in small groups and those who do not. As our church increases in size, our care delivery system will continually become smaller and more personalized. We value the personal touch in ministry.

The following definition encompasses the position of the lay pastor:

LAY PASTOR is one who has the pastoral gift, who is trained and released to do the work of pastoring while still being employed in full-time secular work, and who is not necessarily ordained as an elder.

We believe the information in this manual will help you to transform your church into a dynamic, lay pastor-driven church which effectively meets the needs of your congregation. Whether your church is large or small, the principles and strategies provided here will give you practical instructions to train and mobilize men and women to shepherd your flock.

May the Lord richly bless your ministry as you endeavor to extend the Kingdom!

Equipping the Saints,

Pastor Frank Damazio

Testimonies

Testimonies from Lay Pastors

Randy & Lynnette Thomas

Even amidst busy, hectic schedules, we always looked forward to our Lay Pastor Training class with Pastor Frank. We enjoyed hearing from his heart, and he inspired greater service and excellence within us, along with an increased desire to train up others as well.

As lay pastors, we enjoy great freedom and expression of ministry with support and safety through our relationship with a district elder, an intregal part of the success of our Lay Pastor Program. The lay pastor ministry has ignited a greater sense of passion, fulfillment, and purpose in our lives.

Darrel W. Benton

Tierre and I both feel like we received a part of Pastor Frank as he imparted his vision for the church to us. The Lay Pastor Training class was inspirational and a real down to earth way to learn the responsibilities of pastoring.

Ken Callahan

I appreciated hearing Pastor Frank's heart and vision for the future of our church on a leadership level. The candid and open discussion of the keys to that vision was exciting, inspiring, and left a deposit of faith in my spirit. Issues such as culture, church growth, pastoring, touching our city, prayer, and equipping others for ministry had a real impact on me as they were presented.

Steve & Becky Scheidler

My wife and I have been involved in various forms of ministry in Bible Temple for over 15 years. Prior to Pastor Frank's introduction of the Lay Pastor Program, we always felt we could never really be free to minister to the body or be accepted as leaders unless we were officially "on staff." As a career person who feels called to business, this seemed to be a no-win situation.

Action Ideas

The Lay Pastor Program has been an answer to prayer in that it has removed the "shame" of pursuing a secular profession and given us the freedom, confidence, and authority to move out and minister in a way we could only have imagined a few years ago.

It really "fits" for us and completes the picture. It recognizes our secular calling as a ministry of its own while allowing us to be involved in direct ministry within the local church as well.

Mike White

Being a lay pastor is one of the greatest rewards of my Christian life. It allows me to do the work of shepherding people with confidence and authority while continuing to prosper in the field of business.

With Pastor Damazio's Lay Pastor Program I didn't have to choose between my gifts in business and my call to pastoring.

David & Judy Chown

My appointment to be a lay pastor demonstrated to me that my leaders trusted me and recognized the gift of God in me. Their trust has released a grace, boldness, and confidence into my life that I never knew before. Their confidence in me has also motivated me to stir and release the gift of God in others. To me, this is how the Body of Christ was always ment to be: leaders raising up new leaders, who in turn seek out and release others in service. As a business man, pastor, father, and friend, I want, more than ever, to fulfill the call of God for every role, every job, and every person He sends my way.

Action Ideas

Testimonies from District Pastors

District Pastor - Joel Hjertstedt

Jesus said, "I will build my church," and He is doing it! What an exciting time to be alive and to be co-laborers in what He is doing in these days.

There are several philosophies of pastoring churches. One of the most popular is the evangelistic style in which all the pastoring is done from the pulpit to the pew on Sunday mornings. Another popular style is the nurturing church style which endeavors to minister to and meet the needs of each individual in the congregation. We have chosen to go towards a nurturing, relational style and yet maintain an evangelistic vision for the unsaved and our city.

As a pastor, if your desire is to have a nurturing church, then it is imperative that you have a vision for raising up lay leadership (non-staff) from within your congregation. For as you grow it becomes impossible to keep from adding paid pastors and/or elders to the staff, unless you are simply independently wealthy with an unlimited amount of available funds. Because of this, Bible Temple is using the Moses/Jethro principle—we are raising up lay pastors to work with the district pastors in shepherding the flock of God.

Being a district pastor, I am over two districts which include about 1200 people with whom I serve. Unfortunately, I could never touch all those people by myself and was constantly becoming frustrated trying to do so. I found myself doing only crisis counseling, and barely keeping up with that. I never had time to do the fun and important part of pastoring— dropping in on someone just to see how they are doing, blessing them not just because they called me to come because they were sick.

Implementing the Lay Pastor Program has done a number of wonderful things. First of all, it has freed up my time so that I can spend more time spotting, developing and releasing leaders. Secondly, we are seeing a fulfillment of Ephesians 4:11-16 in that the gifts that God has given to the body are being developed and trained, allowing people to actually do the work of the ministry! There is no greater fulfillment for me than to see someone who has a true pastor's heart be able to pastor people and use the gifts God has given them, instead of sitting on the sidelines not reaching their full potential in Christ.

Action Ideas

Third, we are careful to choose lay pastors because of the true pastor's heart, not just because they are nice people; therefore, the congregation has accepted them as pastors. Now these lay pastors can accompany us in ministering to the body with prayer, counseling, and baptizing, as well as marrying and burying.

Fourth, our Lay Pastor Program has made it possible for us to know the true state of the flock (Proverbs 27:23). Seven of my eleven lay pastors have each been given the responsibility of overseeing four to five small home groups. These lay pastors can then be constantly looking for, spotting, developing, and raising up new small group leaders. They also respond to the needs that arise within those small groups and only send to me the extremely difficult cases or those that need additional assistance.

The other four lay pastors are over given geographical areas from which our membership is drawn. These lay pastors call on and meet the needs of those members who are not involved in small groups. Now we, as district pastors, are living longer, have less ulcers, and actually love what we do! I think that the Lay Pastor Program is and will continue to be a great and invaluable success!

District Pastor - Larry Knox

As a New Testament church we are committed to modeling the outline of Ephesians 4: 11, "It was He who gave some to be apostles, some to be prophets, some to be evangelists, and some to be pastors and teachers, to prepare God's people for works of service, so that the body of Christ may be built up . . ." The Lay Pastor Program alone has allowed us to fulfill our gifting as pastors and it has been with great joy that I can multiply myself into the lives of others and see them fulfill their callings, as they do the work of the ministry. What a pleasure it is to see, after just a short time, my spiritual grandchildren carrying on the ministry of which I've been called. The ability to pastor has been multiplied many times over and has resulted in a better cared for flock.

District Pastor - Bob Isabell

We implemented the Lay Pastor Program in January, 1995. Since January, the program has increasingly gained more popularity with the district pastors, the lay pastors, and the congregation. Before this time, it is sad to say, the district elders were unable to contact people unless it was an emergency or a special need. I had no hope of ever visiting everyone in my district, especially now that I have approximately 1,000 people for whom I am supposed to care. I am compelled to admit that I was feeling like a failure and was so overwhelmed with an ever-growing responsibility that I could not keep up the pace. So with that I actually was becoming demoralized.

This program has brought new excitement, new vision and a breath of fresh air to the pastoral staff. We decided to call these couples "lay pastors" because it ties the people together with the pastoral leadership. It helps everyone to overcome the gap between the people and the pastors. (Like it or not, the gap was there, and it was growing larger.) These couples were chosen from the laity and trained for over a year with a pastoral (shepherd, caring, relating) philosophy. Some had been to Bible school but were doing little with their training. Some had actual pastoral experience but for many reasons found themselves back again at Bible Temple. Many were regular working people and business owners who had a heart for others. One fact that was clear about every couple was that they had a strong call to love and work with people, whether they ever were full time in the ministry or not.

We call these couples "lay pastors" because they were chosen from the laity and want to keep their jobs because they don't feel called to a full time position in the church. We call them "pastors" because they have pastoral hearts and they do hands-on pastoral care. These couples have a genuine pastoral call (some noted through presbytery).

We decided for the first year to limit their time involvement to 3-5 hours per week so that they were not over-burdened. It doesn't seem like much time, but when you multiply 3-5 hours a week by 24 couples, then you realize how much more time is really given to caring for people. There is just no way for us, as district pastors, to ever be able to do this much work, be husbands, be fathers, and be great employees. This is the reason for the feeling of failure that I spoke of previously.

Action Ideas

We have divided the lay pastors into two categories: lay pastors over small groups and lay pastors over non-small groups. The lay pastors over small groups are over 3-5 small groups. A small group consists of 12-35 people, so the lay pastor would average about 80-125 people for whom he now is responsible. He also trains the small group leaders.

Remembering that we now give small groups, small group leaders, and lay pastors a much higher profile than ever before, the people follow the chain of command and actually feel better about it because they know that someone will attend their need much more quickly than in the past. This alone makes this program work.

We also have non-small group lay pastors. They have the responsibility of calling and inviting into their homes people who, for whatever reason, were out of our working system and because of this probably would never get a pastoral call. These lay pastors are responsible for approximately 80-100 people who can be touched 2-4 times a year instead of not at all. Many of these people have already responded with joy and surprise when they were contacted because they either had never been called before or it had been years since a pastor had contacted them.

So far the program has taken a big load off my shoulders as well as my wife's shoulders. We are now getting to do more of what we have been called to do but didn't have the time to do it—train and mentor new couples for leadership. We spend more time with our leaders (lay pastors) than we thought we could. We love it and so do they. One good thing that is coming out of this is the close friendships we are making with new and young leaders. Because we give them a lot of honor, respect, attention, time, and love, they support us and Pastor Frank like never before. As far as I'm concerned, this program has saved our lives!

AY PASTOR
Training Manual

Touch Points for Spiritual Bonding

Action Ideas

Touch Points For Spiritual Bonding

To work together as a team requires a common link: the same view, the same principles, and the same spirit. By "spirit" I am referring to the unity of heart, mind, and soul that takes place when leaders are spiritually bonded together. This spiritual unity is the foundation for building a leadership team.

As the Senior Pastor of Bible Temple, I feel that healthy relationships between my wife and I, and the eldership, lay pastors, and their spouses are an essential ingredient in accomplishing our vision.

I.   NUMBERS 11:16-17 - PRINCIPLES OF LEADERSHIP

Numbers 11:16-17

A. Leaders Should Desire to Share Their _____.

To share their heart means that leaders should demonstrate transparency, vulnerability, and open and honest exposure of both their personal and ministerial lives.

B. Leaders Should Desire to Share Their _____.

To share their burden means that leaders allow others to take ownership and responsibility to understand the real load of ministry along with the real joys and fulfillment.

C. Leaders Should Desire to Share Their _____.

To share vision means that leaders should inspire a bright hope for the future. Vision is something to be caught, not just taught. It is the transferring of spirit, attitude, and heart.

D. Leaders Should Desire to Share Their _____.

To share their shepherd's heart means that leaders should impart deep love, compassion, and concern for people that is foundational to all areas of ministry.

II.   THE JOHN 12:24 PRINCIPLE OF LEADERSHIP

John 12:24

A. The Journey of Death to Ownership

1.   The church is God's church, not mine. Ownership belongs only to our Lord Jesus. We are only stewards and servants. We are to die to self and to our own strengths and ideas.

2.   The vision is God's vision, not mine. If we serve another man's vision with respect, carefulness, and passion, our own vision will be fulfilled.

B. The Maturity of Serving Another Man's Vision

All leadership must be willing to make another persons vision and ministry successful, even to the point of the disciple surpassing his teacher in ministry capabilities. This true-test is best illustrated in Barnabas' selfless ministry philosophy in raising up the apostle Paul.

C. The Grace-Life That Builds Godly People

Grace driven leadership will not minister out of their own mind or their own ideas, but will freely dispense the grace of Christ on all people. Grace is the foundation of working long term in building godly people.

Lay Pastor

Training Manual

Our Vision Statement

Our Vision Statement

Bible Temple Sample

I.   UNDERSTANDING THE BIBLICAL VISION

Proverbs 29:18; Habakkuk 2:2-4

A. Our Vision

1.   To exalt the Lord by dynamic, Holy Spirit-inspired worship, praise, and prayer, and to give our time, talents, and gifts as an offering to the Lord.

2.   To equip the Church to fulfill her destiny through godly vision, biblical teaching, and pastoral ministries. To bring believers to maturity and effective ministry in Christ, resulting in a restored, triumphant Church.

3.   To extend the Kingdom of God from the church to our cities, our nations, and the world through aggressive evangelism, and to train leaders, send out missionaries and mission teams, and plant churches.

B. Our Vision Values

1.   **God's Word:** We believe the Bible is God's inspired Word, the authoritative and trustworthy guideline for the faith and behavior of all Christians.

2.   **God's manifested presence:** To enjoy God's presence is our passion as a church. We believe there is a presence of God available to God's people as we follow the pattern of worship of Psalms.

       Psalm 22:3

3.   **Holy Spirit activity:** In both our personal and corporate life as believers, we welcome the moving of the Holy Spirit. The baptism of the Holy Spirit and the gifts of the Holy Spirit are part of our basic belief.

Action Ideas

4. **Dynamic spontaneous praise and worship:** The believer's response to God's presence is demonstrated in joyful worship, with clapping, lifting hands, and singing spontaneous songs unto the Lord.

5. **The principle of unity:** Not conformity, but unity of spirit and principle. Unity may include a variety of approaches, yet the same principle and convictions flow together to accomplish one vision.

6. **The holiness of God:** Holiness is not a matter of legalism measured by rules, but a true cleansing of the believer by the power of the Holy Spirit. Holiness is evident by Christian character and conduct. The fruit of holiness is easily seen.

7. **Fervent prayer:** As we pray out loud together in our pre-service prayer time, the voice of prayer itself is heard. This principle of prayer is the motor and the power of our church life. Individual praying, as well as fasting and prayer for the whole church, is a continual emphasis.

8. **Excellence:** We believe God deserves the best we have to offer. We seek to maintain excellence in everything connected to the work of God.

9. **Relationships:** Our goal is to love one another. We make this practical through gathering in small groups, called "Life Groups." Every believer is thus able to develop deeper relationships with other believers, resulting in mutual encouragement and accountability.

10. **Integrity:** A good character for each believer is absolutely essential. We consider integrity to be of the highest importance. Uprightness, trustworthiness, and transparency are our best foundation stones.

11. **Kingdom of God influence in our culture:** We are to be salt and light to our world. We believe our society and our political and educational systems should be influenced by God's Spirit and Word.

12. **The family:** We express this commitment by our strong emphasis on family in preaching, teaching, and counseling, as well as through home schooling and a K-12 Christian school.

C. Our Vision of the Church We Will Build

1. A powerful church (*Acts 1:8*)

2. A praying church (*Acts 1:14*)

3. A unified church (*Acts 1:14; 2:1*)

4. A Spirit-filled church (*Acts 2:1; 4:38*)

5. A Word church (*Acts 2:42*)

6. A reverent church (*Acts 2:43*)

7. A sharing church (*Acts 2:44-45*)

8. A gathering-together church (*Acts 2:46*)

9. A supernatural church (*Acts 2:44-45*)

10. A fellowshipping church (*Acts 2:46*)

11. A happy church (*Acts 2:46*)

12. A worshipping church (*Acts 2:46; 15:15-17*)

13. A likable church (*Acts 2:47-48*)

14. A witnessing church (*Acts 1:8*)

15. A growing/expanding church (*Acts 2:42-48*)

16. A missionary-sending church (*Acts 13:1-6; 15:36*)

17. A leadership-training church (*Acts 4,11,13,15*)

18. A society-influencing church (*Acts 17:6*)

Action Ideas

19. A church with elders and deacons (*Acts 6:1-7; 14:23; 16:1-10; 16:4; 20:17*)

20. A church with the gifts of the Holy Spirit (*I Corinthians 12,14*)

II.   UNDERSTANDING THE DISTINCT MISSION

A. An Ephesians 4:11-16 Mission

To win the unchurched and to assimilate them into a committed body of Spirit-filled Christians; to equip people under the leadership of qualified ministers, enabling them to fulfill their God-given purpose; to achieve a level of growth and maturity in these Christians that they may influence the community, the state, and the world.

B. Our Mission Goals

1. To see our church become the church God desires in our area, a church that can reap a great harvest in our city.

2. To see our Christian school facilities enlarged as necessary to train even more young people; to raise up our youth to be people of influence in their generation.

3. To increase and update our Bible college facilities as necessary in order to train more young leaders to take their cities for Christ.

4. To send and support missionaries to foreign fields to be church planters, Bible college teachers, Bible translators, etc.

5. To aid in the planting of churches, both in the United States and internationally.

6. To go on Christian radio and television, sharing our teaching and vision with a great number of people.

7. To translate our books into other languages to reach the world.

8. To become debt free and mortgage free, that we may invest more in training leaders, influencing our city, sending out missionaries, and planting churches.

III.   GRASPING A CLEAR BIBLICAL MINISTRY PHILOSOPHY

Mark 10:38; Luke 14:26-33; Mark 8:34

- A philosophy of ministry that begins with proper personal perspective. The self and all its rights and demands are nailed to the cross, and the Lord becomes the center of one's existence.

- A philosophy of ministry that understands the doctrine of the Body of Christ, authority versus submission, and the concept of accountability. In this way, the Body's health and protection come before personal ambitions, hurts, offenses, and trivial beliefs that might harm the Body.

- A philosophy of ministry that rises out of a personal encounter with God which results, when called by God, in biblical sacrifice and yielding to that call. It is, therefore, a joy and a privilege to give one's life to training and discipleship, to prayer and serving the Body of Christ.

- A philosophy of ministry that demands insight and skills in dealing with potential problem people (Acts 28:3), or people who possess:

  1. *Views, opinions, and concepts that conflict with biblical principles.*

  2. *Hidden expectations or wrong motivations.*

  3. *Disloyalty.*

  4. *Moral impurity.*

  5. *Contentious, divisive spirits.*

  6. *Religiosity or "letter-of-the-law" spirits.*

IV.   STRATEGY AND WISE IMPLEMENTATION

A. Spiritual Ingredients to Implementing Vision

1.   Corporate unity

Joshua 1:2,14; 3:1,17; 4:1,11; Matthew 18:18-19; 12:25; John 17:22

2.   Courageous faith

Joshua 1:6-7,9,18; 2:11; 3:15; 10:25; 23:6; 24:23; 17:17-18; 14:7-11

3.   Commitment to Godly leadership

Joshua 1:5,11,16-18; 3:7,17; 4:14

4.   Sacrificing congregation

Joshua 3-5

5.   "Warrior's" spirit with a conquest strategy

Joshua 5:13-15; 6:1-15; 23:8-10

IN BRIEF, IT COMES DOWN TO:

- Action to Be Taken

- Step of Faith Needed

- Power of God

- Godly Determination

- Godly Commitment

B. Practical Ingredients to Implement Vision

1.   Wise decision making

2.   Wise planning

3.   Financial resources

4.   Sufficient facilities

5.   Strong simple structure

6.   Balanced staffing

V.   BIBLE TEMPLE'S MISSION

- To reach people in the world and to see them become part of Christ's Church.

- To equip and mobilize those people to function fruitfully both in the local church and in every aspect of their lives.

- To take the Kingdom of God into our culture, not the culture of the world into the Church. To resist "culturized" Christianity as a disease that neutralizes the true power of the gospel.

Action Ideas

Twelve Descriptions of a Cutting Edge Church

1990's Society	21st Century Cutting Edge Church	1990's Church General Condition
II Timothy 4:1-2; 3:1-8,13	*The Harvesting Church*	*II Kings 6:5-7* *Revelation 3:14-22*

1. _____

   _____

2. _____

   _____

3. _____

4. _____

5. _____

   _____

6. _____

   _____

7. _____

8. _____

9. _____

10. _____

11. _____

    _____

12. _____

1. _____

   _____

2. _____

3. _____

4. _____

5. _____

6. _____

   _____

7. _____

8. _____

   _____

9. _____

   _____

10. _____

11. _____

    _____

12. _____

    _____

1. _____

   _____

2. _____

   _____

3. _____

   _____

4. _____

5. _____

6. _____

7. _____

8. _____

9. _____

10. _____

11. _____

    _____

12. _____

Action Ideas

The Three-Fold Priority of Vision Fulfillment

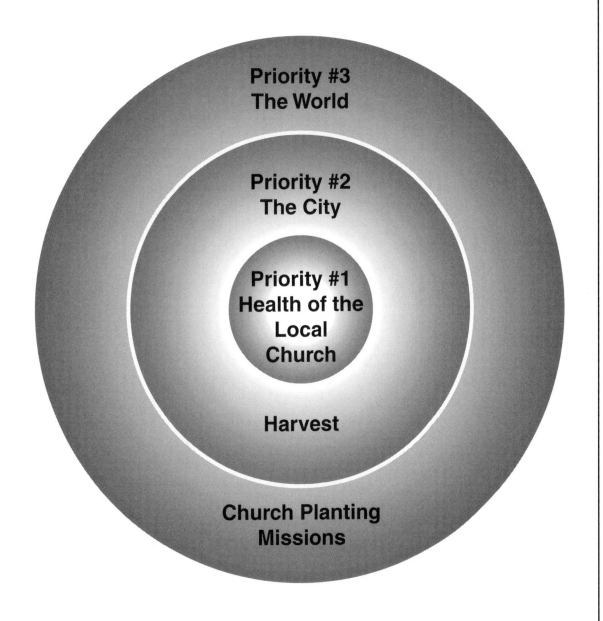

Priority #3
The World

Priority #2
The City

Priority #1
Health of the
Local
Church

Harvest

Church Planting
Missions

The Focus Principle

F ollowing carefully biblical patterns and principles

O vercoming subtle distractions

C ulturally relevant without compromise

U sing time strategically

S eeking supernatural assistance

Five Stages In The Life Cycle Of Churches

	Initial Structuring	Formal Organization	Maximum Efficiency	Institution-alization	Disintegration
Commitment to Mission and Purpose	• Positive, support-ive attitude • Uncertainty of future • Demands vision-ary leader with high commitment level	• Strong sense of mission and pur-pose among mem-bers • High level of goal ownership	• High visibility and understanding of purpose and mis-sion • Common purpose throughout min-istries of the church	• Lowering of mem-bers' understand-ing of purpose • New members do not sense church's purpose	• Purpose is lost • Mission not understood
Involvement of Membership	• Mutual dependen-cy requires every-one to be involved or to leave • All members will-ing to work	• High percentage of individuals' time and identity committed to the church • Volunteers easily found	• New members quickly find a place to become involved • High level of enthusiasm among member-ship for participa-tion	• Members assume there are enough others to do the job • More paid staff to "enhance" min-istries	• Programs elimi-nated for lack of participation • Difficult to find volunteers • 10% of members doing 90% of work
Programs, Structures and Organizations	• Minimal organiza-tion • Spontaneity in disciple-making	• Function of min-istry determines form • Structure created in response to needs • Traditions begin to form	• New programs created to respond to new needs • Delegation begins • New roles and responsibilities created	• Few, if any, new programs added • Forms of min-istries begin to determine func-tion • Structure creates needs rather than responds to needs	• Programs deleted for lack of funds • Primary goal is preservation and survival
Attitude Toward Change	• Members are receptive • Quickly accom-plished • Ownership is unanimous	• Changes easily adopted and inte-grated • Suggested from all levels of member-ship	• New proposals given serious con-sideration • Church leaders responsible for initiating and implementing	• Few changes pro-posed • No changes con-sidered that radi-cally depart from status quo	• "We've never done it that way before" • Rationalizations often made for why it cannot be done
Congregational Morale and Self-esteem	• Morale is high • Self-esteem is in the process of being formulated	• Morale is higher • Self-esteem easily affected by cir-cumstances and short-term suc-cess and failures	• Morale is highest • Self-esteem is at its highest level • Confidence is con-tagious that goals can be reached	• Morale polarizes into groups of high and low • Self-esteem devel-ops uncertainties	• Few have high morale • Frustration and/or despair by leaders in not knowing how to stop decline • Self-esteem lowers

VISION STATEMENT
STRATEGY
STRUCTURE
SCHEDULE
STAFF

TYPE OF STATEMENT	WHAT IT ANSWERS	ITS ORIENTATION
Purpose	Why does the church exist?	Theologically oriented: What is the church's reason for being?
Vision	What is the church supposed to accomplish in ministry?	Seeing oriented: What do we see in our heads as the vision is cast for us?
Mission	What is the church's ministry?	Objective oriented: What does our plan look like?
Philosophy of Ministry	Why do we do what we do?	Value oriented: What shapes our

WHY IS ALIGNMENT IMPORTANT?

An Organization's Direction

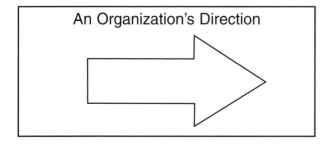

Individual within the Organization

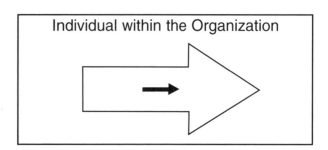

Two People with Different Visions

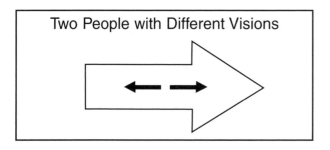

An Aligned Direction

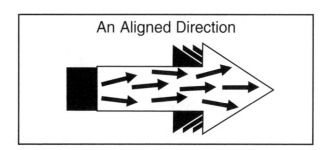

WHAT DOES EFFECTIVE ALIGNMENT LOOK LIKE?

Most Organizations

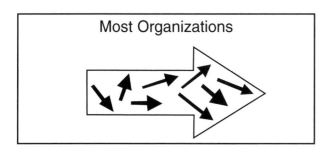

Empowerment in an *Unaligned* Organization

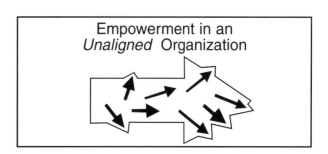

Systems *Not* Aligned with Vision

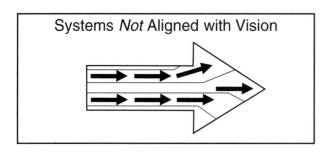

Systems and Structures Aligned with Vision

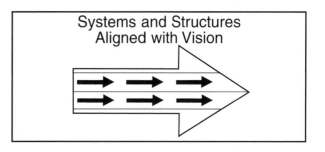

Action Ideas

VI. THE TANGIBLE GOALS OF THE LAY PASTOR PROGRAM

1. To see the harvest reaped, assimilated, and discipled.

2. To develop quality pastors who are prepared and equipped for great regional harvest.

3. To train lay people to do the harvesting and pastoring.

4. To be a meta-church, which includes both a change in church infrastructure and a change of perspective about how ministry is to be done.

5. To become a church with hundreds of lay-led home discipleship centers that multiply remarkably quickly and efficiently.

6. To assure the highest level of care at the lowest level in the structure.

7. To spread ministry responsibilities to qualified lay pastors, utilizing them, but not overburdening any of them. This promotes measurable, low ratio spans of care.

8. To involve every person in a small group, thus enabling them to forge strong links to the church.

9. To ensure leaders' scope of responsibility does not exceed their ability to provide effective care.

10. To promote and honor relationships over programs and methods. Relationships should become the central focus within small groups. Caring for one another is birthed out of love.

11. To mobilize and motivate believers for action, equipping them for effective service.

12. To provide each member a personal pastoral touch via small groups, lay pastors, and district pastors.

13. To establish a structure that pastors the whole church, both small group and non-small group people, and helps the entire church cooperate with the plan.

Action Ideas

14. To teach people that each of them is called to the ministry, in the sense that God has gifted them with spiritual gifts to be used to serve the Body of Christ.

    Romans 12:3-8; I Corinthians 12; I Peter 4:7-11

15. To help people understand what it means to be a minister and to exercise that ministry.

    Mark 10:35-45; I Corinthians 13; I and II Timothy; Titus

16. To help people discover their unique spiritual giftings through teaching on the various gifts, plus questionnaires which will aid in determining spiritual gifts.

17. To help people develop their spiritual gifts and thus equip the saints to do the work of the ministry.

    Ephesians 4:11-12

18. To provide opportunities for people to utilize their spiritual gifts and to get involved in ministry.

    I Peter 4:10

AY PASTOR

Training Manual

The Lay Pastor and the Second Reformation

Action Ideas

The Lay Pastor & The Second Reformation

We are in the midst of a second reformation. The first Reformation put the Scriptures into the hands of the laity. This second reformation puts the ministry into the hands of the laity. I believe that lay people—those outside of the ordained ministries—will be the vanguard of the Holy Spirit's activity in these days.

The layman's traditional role is undergoing scriptural review. In Switzerland in 1974, the Lausanne International Congress on World Evangelism had a laymen's night. A panel of business and professional men discussed the role of laymen in world evangelism. The United States representative, a real estate investor, presented an ultimatum to the gathering. Laymen would no longer be content with the traditional role assigned to them by religious leaders. Traditionally, a good layman was asked to do four things: 1) attend all church functions, 2) give money liberally to church programs, 3) support all church programs established by the leadership, and 4) adhere to the eleventh commandment, "Thou Shalt Not Rock the Boat."

I.   LAY LEADERS IN HISTORY

- **The Waldenses.** In the 12th century, Peter Waldo, a merchant from Lyons, France, wanted to return to the teachings of the New Testament. The Scriptures were translated into the vernacular, and the laity were encouraged to memorize large portions of Scripture. Convinced that laymen could preach the gospel, the movement spread throughout France, Italy, Spain, Germany, and Bohemia. The organized church branded the Waldenses as heretics, and their numbers were scattered and finally dissipated.

- **John Wycliffe.** Wycliffe translated the Latin Vulgate Bible into the language of the people. He taught that laymen could participate in the ministry, even administer the sacraments.

II.   LAY PASTOR PROFILE

- The laity are the vast number of people outside a particular profession. In religious terms, the laity are within the church but not members of the clergy.

- The lay pastor has gifts that have been recognized, trained, and developed by the leadership. Lay pastors do the work of pastoring while still employed full-time in secular work.

- The lay pastor ministry requires recognition of the priesthood of all believers. Each believer has both the right and the responsibility to be an ambassador for Christ and to be a significant minister in Christ's work.

- Kenneth Haughk of Stephen Ministries states, "The priesthood of all believers—lay ministry—drives out all indifference! It develops excitement in the church that multiplies ministry. Congregations that implement a system of intentional training and support of lay ministry become more fully places of love and care, places where the overflowing abundance of God reaches homes, families, and places of work. When the church fails to equip, train, and support its members to be the loving, caring community God calls it to be, indifference and apathy become the norm."

III.   LAY LEADERS IN SCRIPTURE

- **Daniel.** While employed in the political field, Daniel became a spiritual leader to the kings he served. Daniel's prophetic gift gave insight and direction for the events of his day.

- **Nehemiah.** While employed as a cupbearer to the king, he held a high place of honor in the palace of Shushan and had confidential access to the king. At the same time, though in his background he was a prince in Israel, not a priest, he became a pastor/leader to the people of God. He became governor of Jerusalem after rebuilding the walls and restoring the people to divine order.

- **Amos.** The prophet of judgment, Amos is the author of the minor prophet book that bears his name. He was not a professional prophet, did not belong to the order of prophets, nor was he educated in the school of the prophets. He does not appear to have been a man of rank or influence. He was, in fact, a dresser of sycamore trees. He was influenced by the quiet life he led. Time to think and pray enabled him to form clear judgments. The art of a seer is not cultivated in crowds.

- **Priscilla and Aquilla.** This husband and wife were tentmakers who became the Apostle Paul's co-partners in ministry. Paul, also a tentmaker, became close to this awesome couple when he went to Corinth and Athens. He lived with them for eighteen months while establishing a church. Priscilla and Aquilla became strong in discipling, teaching, and hospitality.

- **Onesiphorus.** A lay leader and probably an elder in the church in Ephesus who befriended the Apostle Paul (II Timothy 1:6; 4:19), Onesiphorus opened his house as a center for the ministry. A man with the deep compassion of a pastor's heart, he ministered to Paul, who was undergoing severe trials.

- **Epaphroditus.** Epaphroditus was a lay leader who possessed a commendable character and wonderful pastor's heart (Philippians 2:25; 4:18). He was a co-worker and a fellow soldier to Paul and a man who laid his life on the line to show love and encouragement to others. He was a remarkable person of compassion.

- **Lydia.** Lydia was a very successful businesswoman in the prosperous city of Thyatira (Acts 16:12-15, 40; Philippians 1:9-10). Lydia's home city had many guilds, such as that of "dyers." The city's water was excellent for dying; no other place could produce the scarlet cloth as Thyatira could. This unique purple dye brought the city renown. Lydia was a well-known, very successful seller of this product. She became Paul's first convert, the beginning of the Philippian church.

IV. TRANSITION FROM SHEPHERD TO RANCHER/SHEPHERD

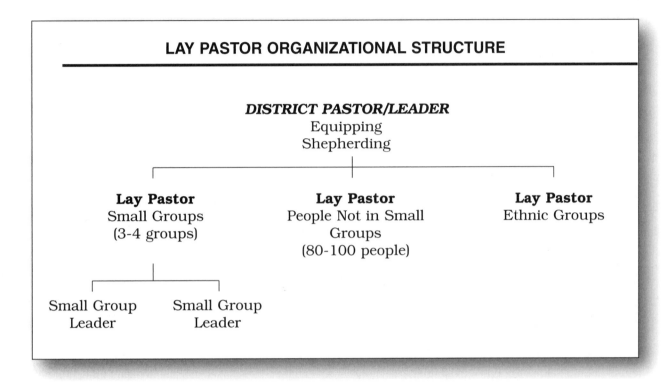

LAY PASTOR ORGANIZATIONAL STRUCTURE

DISTRICT PASTOR/LEADER
Equipping
Shepherding

Lay Pastor
Small Groups
(3-4 groups)

Lay Pastor
People Not in Small
Groups
(80-100 people)

Lay Pastor
Ethnic Groups

Small Group
Leader

Small Group
Leader

A. Ministry and Job Description of a District Pastor and Wife

1. The husband-and-wife team functions together in all areas of pastoral ministry. They follow the Priscilla/Aquilla model of being pastoral ministers, with a love of people, hospitality, and equipping leaders.

2. The husband is a mission-minded leader, with a five-fold level of gifts and abilities to counsel, teach, train, and administer a large group of 1000-2000 people (Ephesians 4:11-12).

3. The wife is a "help meet," and complements with her strength. The wife should have an ability to counsel, an above-average gift in hospitality, ability to assist in administrative needs in the district, to counsel women in the district (especially the young married women), and to help assist in women's ministries, such as teaching ladies' Bible studies and hosting prayer groups in the home.

Action Ideas

4. The husband and wife should both be a force of friendliness and enthusiasm during all services, mingling with people at the front doors, doing altar work, and ministry to people during pre-service prayer. Sunday is their "people day."

5. District pastors as strategists and trainers must:

    a. *Design and administer plans to recruit, develop, train, and encourage group leaders.*

    b. *Create new groups and disciple and equip new leaders.*

    c   *Identify potential small group leaders and oversee their training to enable them to start new small groups.*

    DISTRICT SIZE: 1,000-1,200 People
                                  10 Lay Pastors
                                  50 Small Group Leaders

6. District leadership must be able to:

    a. *Pastor the district through other leaders, while at the same time maintaining a unity of purpose and spirit with the people under those leaders.*

    b. *Draw on strong couples and singles who have the capacity to become pastoral leaders, and then equip them in basic skills.*

    c. *Administer pastoral duties to keep a large district flowing smoothly.*

    d. *Develop administration skills, even though they may not come naturally or be of special interest. Every pastor must confront the challenge of administration as a means to ministry.*

    Old English Word: $\dfrac{\text{Administry}}{\text{Toward Ministry}}$

    All tasks contribute to ministry or lead toward ministry. In this sense, the work of ministry is inseparable from certain tasks of administration.

    e. *Practice hospitality in a big way.*

Action Ideas

    f.   *Utilize people skills, especially in Sunday services. Pastoral friendliness is utterly essential. You are the heart of the church.*

7.   District pastors and wives liaison with leadership

    a.   *District pastors and their wives will meet weekly with their pastor or a designated leader for times of prayer, discussion, and spiritual input.*

    b.   *District pastors, along with the senior pastor, will prepare a systematic plan to equip lay pastors, including use of curriculum, schedules, and goal dates.*

    c.   *District pastors' vision for pastoral ministry includes aggressive goals for growth. Every small group will be taught and motivated to grow. The district pastor and his wife are keys to the vision. Begin to think of one-thousand-people districts, with 10-20 lay pastors, and 50-75 small groups. Start thinking this way now!*

B. Ministry of Lay Pastors

1. _____. Interact with more than one group to provide information, to facilitate, communicate, problem-solve, and encourage.

2. _____. Engage in pastoral ministry counseling on most of the problems people encounter. The lay pastor will ask assistance or transfer moral cases and matters involving child abuse, homosexuality, divorce, divorce/remarriage, and offenses causing someone to leave the church.

3. _____.

4. _____.

5. See to it that group leaders of small groups _____

_____.

6. Help small group leaders _____

_____.

7. Provide the small group leaders with _____

_____ .

8. Ensure that small group leaders _____

_____ .

9. Build up small group leaders by _____

_____ .

C. Ministry of Small Group Leaders

1. Be a facilitator. Facilitate and lead groups designed by others, using the materials designed for small groups. Small group leaders must be trained:

    a. *In the clear purpose of small groups and the goals and four-fold purpose and vision of the church.*

    b. *In the recruitment of new people.*

    c. *In leading a meeting, following material, communication skills, leading discussions. Learn to Pray—Prepare—Guide—Care.*

    d. *In common care counseling.*

    e. *In leadership styles (i.e., domineering, authoritative, democratic).*

    f. *To recognize obstacles to effective leadership.*

2. Make a two to three year commitment.

3. Serve twelve to twenty people.

V.   FOUR-FOLD PURPOSE OF SMALL GROUPS

FOUR-FOLD PURPOSE OF SMALL GROUPS

Relationship

- Friendship development
- Honest sharing
- Fellowship—developing a community spirit
- Shared life, meals, time
- Accountability

Pastoral Care

- Accepting and belonging
- Support
- Crisis help
- Counseling availability
- A supportive environment for struggle, change, and decision

Equipping

- Context for discovery, deployment of your spiritual gift
- Context for developing lay leadership
- Context for Christian ministry
- Context for encouraging every believer to become a disciple of Christ
- Context for training new leaders

Evangelism

- Mobility and flexibility
- Informality
- Freedom
- Faith is contagious
- Training in witnessing
- Strategic growth

The Lay Pastor and Vision for the City

Action Ideas

The Lay Pastor & Vision for the City

We must lift ourselves out of a self-centered spirituality, a mentality that says we are victims rather than warriors. Our vision must be God's vision. Our mission is to reach our cities and make them places where God's presence, God's ways, and God's Word flourish.

Over half the world's population lives in urban centers and large cities. Most of those cities are filled with violence, drugs, gangs, prostitution, poverty, and perversion. We are called to these cities, not because they are beautiful or the best places to raise children, but because God has called us there. We must see our city and region as it really is, not merely as it appears to be. Our vision for missions must also focus on cities.

God has a vision for our cities to become places of shelter, communion, purity, and hope. We must understand God's sovereign purpose for our cities. We need a vision of hope. We must speak positive words and cease denouncing the city and being negative about certain problems.

Let us begin to proclaim God's prophetic destiny for our cities. What do we expect Him to do specifically in our cities? Is our vision too small?

Our God is only as big as what we expect of Him in time and space!

Romans 5:20; Jeremiah 29:7; Isaiah 58:12; Proverbs 29:18; Isaiah 40:1-2

I.   THE CHURCH IN THE CITY

A. God's Perspective of the Church in the City

Matthew 16:16-18

1.   Biblical definition of Christ's Church

II Corinthians 8:1; Galatians 1:2; Revelation 1-3

a.   *We acknowledge "the church" in "the city" refers to the whole Church. The Church is made up of all congregations which believe in the New Testament definition of the Church.*

    b.   *Christ's Church is the Universal Church.*

        Acts 20:28; Ephesians 5:32

        Not national, international, denominational, non-denominational, sectarian, or non-sectarian: it is one new man, a new thing!

2.   The focused perspective

    II Corinthians 11:18

    a.   *We acknowledge the local church and each individual congregation of believers has bishops, deacons, and saints. There are a variety of congregations, but one Church!*

    b.   *Ekklesia: "'Called out to assemble together'; an organism, assembly, congregation, the local church."*

B. The Proper Perspective of Local Churches in the City

    Revelation 1-3

The seven churches of Asia reveal several truths:

1.   Each local church has its own _____.

    Romans 8:28-29; Luke 19:44

2.   Each local church has its own _____.

We are not to compare or judge another church because it is different. We are not to judge anyone.

3.   Each local church has its own _____.

We are to accept this as a practical outworking of the church vision, the pastoral ministry, and the shaping power of the Holy Spirit.

4.   Each local church has its own _____ which is a reflection of its doctrinal/biblical distinctives, as well as the unique church history background and present leadership. Each church is different, not wrong or unbiblical because it is unique.

II. GOD'S RELATIONSHIP TO THE CITY

A. God Hears the Cry of the City.

1. Genesis 18:20-21: "And the LORD said, 'Because the outcry against Sodom and Gomorrah is great, and because their sin is very grave, I will go down now and see whether they have done altogether according to the outcry against it that has come to Me; and if not, I will know.'"

2. If we could tune in to the "cry" of our cities, what would we hear? Would we hear the cry of the unborn, the abused, the youth without a father or mother, the homosexual who hates his life, the wealthy who are desperately dissatisfied with life, the alcoholic contemplating suicide, or the mother violated through rape and now dying of AIDS?

B. God Weeps Over the City.

Luke 19:41-44

C. God Speaks to the City.

Micah 6:9; Proverbs 1:20-21; 8:1-3

D. God Sends Ministries to Cities.

Jonah 1:2; Luke 9:51-56

III. EVALUATING BIBLICAL MODELS OF MINISTRY TO THE CITY

A. The Nehemiah Model: A Deep Spiritual Burden for the City

Nehemiah 1:1-4

1. Nehemiah heard the report of his city. In response, he spent four months of fasting, praying, weeping, and mourning.

2. Nehemiah developed a vision of restoration.

a. *Walls: morality, families*

Action Ideas

        b.   Gates: authority, order

   3.   Nehemiah witnessed firsthand the terrible condition of the city.

   4.   Nehemiah purposed to arise, restore, and rebuild.

B. The Pauline Model: A Melting of His Spirit for the City

   1.   Acts 17:16 (Athens)

        a.   Amplified: "His spirit was grieved and roused with anger as he saw this city."

        b.   Phillips: "His soul was exasperated at the sight of the city when he saw the city given over to idols."

   2.   Acts 19:21 (Jerusalem, Rome): "When these things were accomplished, Paul purposed in the Spirit, when he had passed through Macedonia and Achaia, to go to Jerusalem, saying, 'After I have been there, I must also see Rome.'"

C. The Acts Model: A Key for Every City

A KEY FOR EVERY CITY	
City	*The Key*
Sychar, John 4:28-30, 39-42	_____
Jerusalem, Acts 1-4	_____
Samaria, Acts 8	_____
Joppa, Acts 9:36-42	_____
Caesarea, Acts 10	_____
Antioch, Acts 11	_____
Lystra, Acts 14	_____
Philippi, Acts 16	_____
Thessalonica, Acts 17	_____
Corinth, Acts 18	_____

IV.   THE DIVINE KEY FOR PENETRATING CORINTH

A. The Corinthian City

1. **A Port City:** a seaman's paradise, a drunkard's heaven, a virtuous woman's hell

2. **An Immoral City:** Temple of Aphrodite, only thousand male and female prostitutes

3. **An Educational City:** arts, sciences, languages

4. **A Sports City**

5. **A Hedonistic City**

6. **A Mixed Race City**

B. Corinthian City Promise—Our Promise

Acts 18:9-10: "Now the Lord spoke to Paul in the night by a vision, 'Do not be afraid, but speak, and do not keep silent; for I am with you, and no one will attack you to hurt you; for I have many people in this city.'"

C. Corinthian Key—Our Key

I Corinthians 2:1-1

V.   ARTICULATING A FUTURE STRATEGIC PLAN - A Bible Temple Sample

• Our strategic plan is to maintain a strong local church with spiritual armory, able to penetrate the spiritual powers "over" or "in" our city.

Jeremiah 50:25

• Our strategic plan is to reap the harvest God would give us from our city area, using every means available or necessary.

Matthew 9:35-37

Action Ideas

- Our strategic plan is to mobilize the local church members throughout our city area through small groups which are structured to reach every neighborhood with the love of God.

    Acts 2:37-47

- Our strategic plan is to penetrate every pocket or stronghold of darkness by increasing the ministry of intercessory prayer and corporate prayer.

    Genesis 18:22-23; Isaiah 59:16

- Our strategic plan is to help restore the inner city by reaching individuals with Christ, so that youth, singles and families can be established in the church.

    Isaiah 58:12; Isaiah 61:4

- Our strategic plan is to oppose moral perversity, homosexuality, pornography, prostitution—all moral sins that violate God's Word—by being salt and light and, as necessary, by political involvement.

    Isaiah 58:19

- Our strategic plan is to train spiritual leaders in our churches to become dynamic leaders in the workplace, in business, and in the church.

    Genesis 14:13; Psalm 87:1-7

- Our strategic plan is to launch more public ministries into our city through teams for street ministry, through downtown and intensified city-wide ministries, and through music, drama, and concerts.

    Acts 1:1-8

The Lay Pastor and the Jethro Principle

The Lay Pastor & The Jethro Principle

Like most who are called to the pastorate, Moses had a heart for his people. Like most congregations, the people had needs. For Moses to find the balance between his heart and his people's needs required wisdom, foresight, and the ability to delegate authority. As Moses did, we must first understand the ministry gift God has given us before we can release that gift to others. Moses' dilemma and his method of solving it provide valuable insights for us.

I.   MOSES ENCOUNTERS SHEPHERDING DILEMMA

Exodus 18:13-18; Numbers 11:10-15

A. Too Many Problems for One Man to Handle

   Exodus 18:13-16

B. Too Heavy a Load for One Man to Carry

   Exodus 18:18; Numbers 11:14-15; Exodus 38:26

   "Thou wilt surely wear away."

   "This thing is too heavy for thee."

   "Thou may not be able to perform it thyself alone."

II.   MOSES ENRICHED BY WISE COUNSEL

Exodus 18:19

A. Qualifications for the Chosen Leaders

   Exodus 18:21-22

   _____

   Hebrew: "To have strength, power, might, especially to be warlike; to display courage, valor; to be firm."

   _____

   Hebrew: "Reverencing God." Fearing and proper living are closely related, almost synonymous.

Action Ideas

Hebrew: "Secure, certain, stability; consistent in performing promises; man of his word, integrity."

Not moved by financial gain.

Wisdom is needed in leadership and in every area of life (see Proverbs).

Proven in their ministries, reputation established, accepted by the people.

B. Responsibilities of Chosen Leaders

MOSES ENRICHED BY WISE COUNSEL

Exodus 18:19; Deuteronomy 1:9-18; Numbers 11:17,24-25,29;
Ecclesiastes 4:9-12; Proverbs 11:14; 15:22; 24:6

Moses' Responsibilities	_Support Leaders' Responsibilities_
Exodus 18:19	_Numbers 1:52_
Exodus 18:20	_Exodus 18:21-22_
Exodus 18:21; _Numbers 11:17,25_	_Exodus 18:22_
Exodus 18:22	_Exodus 18:22_
Exodus 14:15-16	_Exodus 17:9-16;_ _Numbers 16:1-11; 17:5,8-9_

C. The Leaders Moses Chose

Numbers 1:1-17

1. Elizur: "God the rock; strength."

   _____

2. Shelumiel: "Peaceful, happy, friendly, healthy."

   _____

3. Nahshon: "To diligently observe."

   _____

4. Nethneel: "Given of God" (tribe of Issachar the servants).

   _____

5. Eliab: "God of his fathers; might."

   _____

6. Elishama: "God hearing, to hear intelligently, obedient."

   _____

7. Coamaliel: "Reward of God; to treat a person well."

   _____

8. Abidan: "Father of judgment; umpire."

   _____

9. Ahiezer: "Brother to help; to aid, strength."

   _____

10. Pagiel: "Wounded of God."

    _____

11. Eliasaph: "God is harvesting; a worker who continues."

    _____

12. Ahira: "Brother of wrong; adversity, affliction."

    _____

D. The Moses Lay Pastor Structure

600	leaders of 1,000
6,000	leaders of 100
12,000	leaders of 50
60,000	leaders of 10
78,600	leaders

III. HISTORICALLY SUCCESSFUL SMALL GROUPS

A. Moravians (Bandon)

Small groups of people, eight to twelve in each group.

B. Wesley (Nurture Cells)

Wesley called this his foundation for lasting results of evangelism and discipleship. Eight to twelve people were in each group.

C. Holiness Movement (Church in the Home)

This was the grass roots of their movement, because Holiness was better explained and taught in small groups.

D. Cho (Korea) (Home Cell Groups)

Ten to twelve units, or households, in each group. When a unit reaches thirteen households, they form a new group.

E. New Testament Church

Acts 2:46; 12:12; 17:5

Action Ideas

IV.   THE ADVANTAGES OF SMALL GROUPS

A. Small Groups Provide:

1. A framework to bring practical, consistent, and systematic changes in the lives of those under your care.

2. An atmosphere where people can be rooted and grounded together in genuine relationships.

3. An opportunity for people to learn inter-dependence, not dependence.

4. An opportunity for each member to bear the burdens and needs of other members.

5. The framework to give and receive encouragement.

6. The framework for warning and correction.

7. A haven for security and refuge.

8. The opportunity to exhort one another.

9. A training ground for ministry and evangelism.

V.   THE METRO CHURCH

Large stores, companies, and corporations are admired. As a business expands, it is able to offer better options and prices. Huge corporations such as IBM, GMC, and AT&T can afford to do extensive research, set standards, and supply superior products and services. Patients requiring hospital care obviously prefer large, well-established, modern facilities to struggling little clinics. For long-distance flights, no one takes a single engine plane that dusts crops along the way. Yet for some reason, large churches are suspect. The pastor is assumed to be too concerned about numbers or buildings.

Action Ideas

Neighborhood Church / Metro Church: A Contrast

Neighborhood Church Concept *Acts 1:15*	*Metropolitan Church Concept* *Acts 2:41,47; 4:2; 6:1-4*
• 10-300 members	• 300-100,000 members
• One big family where everyone knows everyone because it is easy to know everyone.	• One big, huge extended family where you know your group, and lots of faces.
• The pastor is pastor to everyone. He does almost everything because there is no other staff. The people want him to be available and lovable.	• It is impossible to have one pastor relate to thousands of people. A pastoral ministry team provides a complex yet effective method to minister to this large family.
• Congregation is drawn from the immediate neighborhood area.	• The congregation is drawn from a vast radius and diverse backgrounds.
• There is a tendency for church to become inbred, a one-man operation, with strong centralized loyalty to "our church." Congregation is often resistant to change, and it is difficult to attract new people.	• The church is less inbred, relying on a complex organization of ministries with some specialists. There is a leadership team. It is an "open church," with decentralized leadership.

It is possible to be a metropolitan church with
a neighborhood spirit/atmosphere.

Large churches set trends, have wide influence, and implement innovations. They have a distinctive history, their own unique culture, and are a community within a community.

The Lay Pastor and Team Convictions and Principles for Spiritual Success

Action Ideas

The Lay Pastor & Team Convictions & Principles for Spiritual Success

I.   TEAM MEMBERS' CONVICTIONS SHOULD BE:

- A conviction that God has placed them where they are for His pleasure and purpose and for their good.

- A conviction that places Christ and His people above all of the leaders' own desires, ambitions, and opinions. Team members must see the ministry as a way to serve and to give rather than as a way to fulfill or promote themselves.

- A willingness to accept any assignment necessary to advance the team's overall vision. A team member must reject position-consciousness or an others-should-thank-me, recognize-me, or reward-me attitude. A servant becomes great by making others successful. Therefore, a team member must come with a servant's spirit and a servant's heart, having the overall vision of the church in mind.

- A conviction of loyalty that will save the church and the team in a time of testing. This conviction can only be proven when there is disagreement, disappointment, or disillusionment.

- A conviction of faithfulness. The faithful team member understands promotion comes from the Lord and the Lord promotes based on His principles. The principles of faithfulness and integrity are basic to leadership.

- A conviction of availability. Team members see availability as the needed ingredient to being a useful vessel to God, to other leaders, and to those being served. Being available requires good discipline of time and priorities.

Action Ideas

II. TEAM LEADERSHIP'S POTENTIAL PROBLEMS

- The Problem of Doctrinal Compatibility

- The Problem of Disloyalty in Attitude and Action

- The Problem of Divisive Philosophical Differences

- The Problem of Prejudging Actions By Questioning Motives

- The Problem of Allowing Disciples to Praise Some and Devour Others

- The Problem of Becoming Position-Minded

- The Problem of Those Who Over-Estimate Their Own Abilities and Ministries

- The Problem of Disappointment and Criticism Resulting From Unmet Expectations in Relationships

- The Problem of Ignoring Basic, Established, Agreed-Upon Standards and Core Beliefs

Resource material from: Chapter Twenty-Nine "The Leadership and the Set Man" of **Effective Keys To Successful Leadership** *by Frank Damazio—available through BT Publishing.*

The Lay Pastor's Personal and Pastoral Prayer Life

The Lay Pastor's Personal & Pastoral Prayer Life

Colossians 1:9-12

In this passage in Colossians, we see Paul pour a rush and fervor into his prayer. None of his writings are so lofty and impassioned, none reveal his soul so clearly, as when he turns from speaking *of God to men* to speaking *to God for men.* On his knees, he pastors us.

I.　PAUL'S PRAYER LIFE

A.　Paul's Example of Praying

1.　_____

"For this cause" (Colossians 1:9)

a.　*He prays specifically in response to the news from Colossi.*

b.　*He centers his prayer on the specific issue.*

2.　_____

"Ceased not" (Colossians 1:9)

a.　*Constant and fervent*

b.　*II Thessalonians 1:22; I Thessalonians 5:17*

3.　_____

"To pray for you" (Colossians 1:9)

a.　*Paul prays from prison, while in difficult situations.*

b.　*Paul prays for the Colossians' needs, not his own.*

Action Ideas

4. _____

    a.   *Paul prays for a spiritual blessing, not for material or physical matters.*

    b.   *Jude 1:20*

B. Paul at Prayer: The Truth of Bowing Our Knees

    1.   Signifies _____ of prayer

        I Kings 8:54; Acts 7:60; 9:40; Luke 22:41

    2.   Signifies _____ of prayer

        Daniel 6:10

    3.   Signifies _____ of prayer

        Mark 1:40

II.   PETITION FOR TROUBLED BELIEVERS

Colossians 1:9-11

A. Pray and Ask

    1.   Pray *(prosukomai)*: "Beseech, petitionary praying, to vow; to greatly desire; strong wish or feeling." Paul lifted up his desires in prayer.

        Colossians 1:3,9; 4:3; Ephesians 6:18; Acts 14:23; Romans 8:26

    2.   Ask *(aiteo)*: "To demand; to request with a right and authority" (Used in the New Testament regarding an individual's petitions, which constitute a prayer and include a direct request to seek; to turn aside by asking).

        Matthew 7:7-9; 18:19; 21:22; Luke 11:9-13; John 15:7; Ephesians 3:20; I John 5:14-15

Action Ideas

B. Paul's Eight-Fold Prayer Petition

1. "That you may be filled with the knowledge of His will."

    a. *Filled: "Controlled by the full knowledge of God's will."*

    b. *Knowledge: "Deep, accurate apprehension; the foundation of all believers' conduct."*

    c. *Will of God: "What God is intending to do, and what He desires that we should do."*

2. ". . . that you may be filled with all spiritual wisdom and understanding."

    a. *Wisdom: "Knowledge of the eternal truths."*

    b. *Understanding: "Ability to apply these truths to everyday living."*

3. ". . . that you may walk in a manner worthy of the Lord . . ."

    Ephesians 4:1; Philippians 1:27; I Thessalonians 2:12; 4:1; Colossians 2:6

    a. *In our affections: what we deeply desire*

    b. *In our direction: what we truly seek*

    c. *In our dispositions: the set of our wills*

4. ". . . that you may bear fruit in every good work . . ."

    Ephesians 2:10; Titus 1:16; 2:7,14; 3:8

    a. *Bear fruit: "A life that exhibits continual fruitfulness."*

    b. *Every good work: "Active goodness of every kind."*

5. ". . . that you may increase in the knowledge of God . . ."

6. ". . . that you may be strengthened with all power . . ."

    Ephesians 1:19; 3:16

    a. *A continuous renewal and empowerment*

b.   *A many-sided strength and power for all problems, without limitations*

7.   "... that you may patiently endure ..."

a.   *Endurance (hupomone): "The refusal to be daunted by hard times, capacity to see things through."*

b.   *Patience (makrothumia): "The refusal to be upset by perverse people; an attitude that does not retaliate in spite of injury or insult."*

8.   "... that you may be filled with all joy ..."

Galatians 5:22; Philippians 3:1

a.   *Joy: "The cheerful exercise of endurance and forbearance."*

Inner victories of the soul during hardship are just as great, if not greater, than public victories.

*Resource material from: "**Seven Power points of Prayer**" (tape series) and "**Gap Standing and Hedge Building**" (tape series) by Frank Damazio—available through BT Publishing.*

The Lay Pastor's Personal Revival Experience

The Lay Pastor's Personal Revival Experience

The study of Zerubbabel yields several pertinent insights into a leader who had a tremendous vision, yet was in need of personal renewal. His need for personal renewal was not because of personal sin, failure, or lack of spirituality but because of the strenuous work he was called to accomplish. Zerubbabel is a model to be studied for the revival-times leader who must have a very real encounter with the God who called him. By examining the historical setting as well as the prophetic messages, we can gain insight into what brought about renewal in the life of this leader during turning points in history.

I. THE ZERUBBABEL LEADERSHIP PROFILE

A. The Historical Context

Ezra 1-6; Zechariah 1-6; Haggai 1-2

B. Zerubbabel Leadership Profile

1. Leaving familiar ground

Ezra 1:3,5; 2:1-2; Haggai 1:14

2. Identifying ministry priorities

Ezra 3:2-3

3. Proclaiming the breadth of vision

Ezra 3:4-5

4. Making foundation building glorious

Ezra 3:10-13

5. Expecting warfare to match the work

Ezra 4:1-7

6. Experiencing delayed and incomplete vision

Ezra 4:24

Action Ideas

7. Knowing work stopped is not work ended

    Ezra 4:24

II. THE ZERUBBABEL ENCOUNTER WITH THE PROPHETIC SPIRIT

Ezra 5:1-6:14; Zechariah 4:1-6

A. Awakening Sleeping Leadership

    Zechariah 4:1

B. Acknowledging God's Vision for Oil-Filled Churches

    Zechariah 4:2

C. Assimilating God's Prophetic Message

    Zechariah 4:6

1. Mountains of resistance will be leveled like a plain.

    Zechariah 4:6-7; Ezra 4:1-5,24; Isaiah 40:4; 41:15; 49:11; Matthew 17:20; 21:21; Mark 11:23; I Corinthians 13:2

2. Ultimate triumph and completion of the vision is certain.

    Zechariah 4:8-9; Haggai 2:1-9

3. "Small things" and "slow beginnings" are not to be despised.

    Zechariah 4:10

4. Oil-filled leaders must continuously supply the oil for the lampstand.

    Zechariah 4:11-12; Exodus 27:20; 29:40; Leviticus 24:2; Numbers 28:5; Matthew 25:1-10; Luke 10:34; Hebrews 1:9

5. God is sovereign and in control of all matters, including the opposition, pressures, and strange circumstances of the ministry.

    Zechariah 4:11-14

Action Ideas

III.   THE ZERUBBABEL RENEWAL

A. Renewed Leadership Spirit

Ezra 5:2

B. Renewed Vision for the House

Ezra 5:2

C. Renewed Team Spirit: Working With Other Ministries

Ezra 5:11

D. Renewed Confidence as Servants of God

Ezra 5:11

IV.   MODERN ZERUBBABELS: LEADING A CHURCH INTO REVIVAL

- The leadership must be in _____ concerning the biblical stance of any new truth or emphasis introduced and maintained in the local church. Scriptural foundation is necessary.

    Psalm 133:1-3

- The leadership is to _____ into new moves of the Holy Spirit. It is not a necessity for them to have had the same experiences as others in order to lead the church into new truths. Subjective experiences are not to be measured by the experience itself. Leaders are also individuals following the Lord.

- Leaders are to be _____ and open to Holy Spirit uniqueness. They must lead the church in hunger for God and have an attitude of faith and an attitude of expectancy about God and His workings and not analyze everything to death.

- Leaders are to be _____ and protect the flock and the vineyard. But leaders must also be watchmen over their own vineyards, their own souls, and watch their own walls lest they allow anything to be built that could hinder the moving of the Holy Spirit.

Action Ideas

- Leaders are to be _____ in spirit and attitude, desiring to be in the forefront with a "cutting-edge" faith. But being out front has certain hazards. We must be careful, but not fearful.

- Leaders gain _____ when they follow God with obedience and humility and serve people with sincerity and simplicity.

  "You have left the springtime of your love"(Revelation 2:4).

- Leaders are called to be the _____ any and every wall in their own lives that hinders that powerful renewal of the Holy Spirit.

  ". . . He is coming, leaping upon the mountains. . . . He is standing behind the wall, He is looking through windows" (Song of Solomon).

- Leaders are called to _____ to the voice of God, to first be in communion with Him, and then to communicate the voice of God.

  ". . . Let me see your appearance, let me hear your voice. For your voice is sweet, your appearance lovely" (Song of Solomon 2:14).

- Leaders are to _____ to be their portion for the future. "Call unto me, I will answer you, and show you great and mighty things which thou knowest not" (Jeremiah 33:3). "There is a sound of an abundance of rain" (I Kings 18:41). Elijah had prophetic eyes to see the rain. Elijah had prophetic ears to hear the rainfall.

- Leaders are to be _____, but not fearful of visitation or changes in us, in our programs, or in our people. Changes—that are not in distinctives, but in methods and programs and application of truth.

For further resource information refer to: **Seasons of Revival** *and* **Zerubbabel Principle (Tape)** *by Frank Damazio available through BT Publishing.*

The Lay Pastor as Equipper

Action Ideas

The Lay Pastor As Equipper

"And He Himself gave some to be apostles, some prophets, some evange-lists, and some pastors and teachers, for the equipping of the saints for the work of ministry, for the edifying of the body of Christ, until we all come to the unity of the faith and of the knowledge of the Son of God, to a perfect man, to the measure of the stature of the fullness of Christ"
(Ephesians 4:11-13).

I. THE LEADERSHIP'S CALL IS TO BE EQUIPPERS

A. Defining the Word "Equip"

1. Greek *(Katartismos)*: Preparing or training, to complete thorough-ly, to repair, to adjust; a craftsman.

2. *Katartismos* translated:

   *"Going on from there, He saw two other brothers, James the son of Zebedee, and John his brother, in the boat with Zebedee their father, **mending** their nets . . ." (Matthew 4:21).*

   a. _____

   James and John were bringing the broken strands of their nets together with other strands to make the nets function proper-ly. They were mending, adjusting, and equipping the net to do the work of fishing. Those strands had been broken and had to be mended in order to make the nets usable again. What they were doing in the natural was prophetic of what they were destined to do in the spiritual: to mend the church. Jesus had called them to be "fishers of men."

   Mending broken lives is the work of the governmental min-istries to the Body of Christ. Those ministries bring the broken and battered strands together with other strands to make a strong net which will do the work of catching fish—or souls— for Jesus. When the net broke, James and John did not dive into the water and try to catch the fish themselves. They were, rather, restoring what was broken so that the net itself could

function in its work. Many pastors in the Church today try to do the work of the whole Body, instead of fulfilling their ministry of equipping the Body to do the work.

b. _____

"The vessels of wrath fitted to destruction" (Romans 9:22).

Here the Greek word is used to describe the fitting, or forming, of clay into vessels by a potter. God is the potter who is making vessels of honor or vessels of wrath. A person can either respond as pliable clay to the hand of the Lord, or he can reject God's shaping hand. The Lord is the source of all adjustments and corrections. The governmental ministries are His hand to be instruments which the Lord uses to fashion that correction.

c. _____

"Now I plead with you, brethren . . . that there be no divisions among you, but that you be perfectly joined together in the same mind and in the same judgment" (I Corinthians 1:10).

The Corinthian church had been torn within by the spirit of division. The Apostle Paul desired that all the joints and parts of the Body which were out of place in the Body of the Church would come into adjustment. Paul wanted mending to take place in the Body so it would function with perfect coordination. The Church has great need for the five-fold office ministries to be released to their proper function of healing wounds and rebuilding that which has broken down. Only when these ministries fulfill this work in the Body will the Body of Christ ever be "perfectly joined together."

d. _____

"Therefore, when He came into the world, He said: 'Sacrifice and offering You did not desire, but a body You have prepared for Me.'" (Hebrews 10:5).

This passage quotes a Messianic prophecy found in Psalms 46:6. The body "prepared" for Jesus was a human body of flesh and bones, prepared by the Holy Spirit in Mary's womb. When Jesus came into the world, he came into a "prepared" body for the single purpose of doing the Father's will. As a sinless and perfect body was prepared for the Lord Jesus, so God

is preparing a many-membered Body through which His Son is continuing His spiritual ministry on the earth. The Father is using the governmental ministries to prepare and perfect the Body (the Church) so that it can accomplish His eternal purpose of subjugating all things under the feet of Jesus Christ.

e.   _____

"By faith we understand that the worlds were framed by the word of God . . ." (Hebrews 11:3).

Here the writer is not talking about the original act of creating the worlds. This refers to putting in order, arranging, and fitting for use that which already exists. The already-created worlds were set in order by the Word of God. The universe was adjusted, arranged by God's Word. In the same way, the power of the spoken Word of God will enable the governmental ministries to bring the Body of Christ together.

3. Classical Greek usage of *Katartismos*

   a. *Setting in order a city which had been torn apart by factions and schisms*

   b. *Outfitting or preparing a ship for a long journey*

   c. *Preparing an army for battle*

B. Word Pictures to Describe Equippers

   1. _____ of the soldiers in the army of the Lord

   2. _____ of the broken bones of the Body of Christ

   3. _____ of the boards of God's House

   4. _____ of the muscles in Christ's Body

   5. _____ of the stones in the Temple of the Lord

   6. _____ of the breaches in the hedge of God's garden

   7. _____ of those who are bound

   8. _____ of those who are out of joint

9. _____ of those who are torn

10. _____ of the Body of Christ

11. _____ of God's people

12. _____ of the Lord's Kingdom

13. _____ of God's clay vessels

14. _____ of potential for God's service

II. THE LEADERSHIP'S OBSTACLES TO EQUIPPING

A. The Obstacle of Faulty Concepts/Perspectives of Pastors and Leaders

1. If the pastor is "Mr. Superstar," then the church is an audience, not a body.

2. If the pastor is "Mr. Wonderful," then the church acts as if his faith and abilities were theirs.

3. The biblical emphasis is not on the "Omni-competent Pastor" but on a multi-gifted body.

B. The Obstacle of Character/Emotions of Pastors and Leaders

1. The problem with "the more I do the more I'm loved and needed" mind set is that pastors do everything.

2. The problem with insecurity is that it drives pastors to do all the work so as to get all the praise.

C. The Obstacle of Wrong Attitudes Toward Lay People

1. David Watson: "Most Protestant denominations have been as priest-ridden as the Roman Catholics. It is the minister, vicar, or pastor who has dominated the whole proceedings. In other words, the clergy-laity divisions have continued in much the same way as in pre-Reformation times, and the doctrine of spiritual gifts and body ministry have been largely ignored."

Action Ideas

2.   John Stott: "Laity is often a synonym for amateur as opposed to professional, or unqualified as compared to expert."

3.   The church is fundamentally a charismatic community, for the *charismata* (grace gifts) have been distributed to all. This makes each person an initiating center for ministry.

4.   "Lay Person" is a scriptural word filled with dignity and honor. *Laos* portrays a sense of specialness.

> *"For you are a holy people [laos] to the LORD your God; the LORD your God has chosen you to be a people [laos] for Himself, a special treasure above all the peoples on the face of the earth"* (Deuteronomy 7:6).

> *"I will walk among you and be your God, and you shall be My people"* (Leviticus 26:12).

> *"But you are a chosen generation, a royal priesthood, a holy nation, His own special people, that you may proclaim the praises of Him who called you out of darkness into His marvelous light"* (I Peter 2:9).

> *". . . who gave Himself for us, that He might redeem us from every lawless deed and purify for Himself His own special people, zealous for good works"* (Titus 2:14).

5.   A lay person, *laos*, is a new humanity, the vanguard of the future, the prototype of the Kingdom of God not yet completed, a person of the future living in the present. Next time someone says, "I'm just a lay person," we should respond, "That's more than enough!"

III.   EQUIPPING SAINTS: SPIRITUAL AND PRACTICAL APPLICATION

A. Ministry Focus of _____

1.   Our goal should be to fix what is broken. Something is broken when it cannot perform the function for which it was designed. If it is disjointed or disconnected, it must be restored.

2.   Our ministry attitude must first be:

"We take you as you are. Grace is dispensed here."

"We pay attention to brokenness in the lives of people. We mend; we pray; we counsel; we bring healing."

"We are a restoring church. We restore people back to proper working order."

B. Ministry Focus of _____

1.   We must make certain an individual has been properly healed, restored, and brought to a level of maturity. Then he will be able to handle the discipline involved in being discipled and taking responsibility.

2.   We must allow people to discover their aptitudes, abilities, and capacity for ministry. Then we can help them refine their skills.

3.   We must help people discover their spiritual gifts and allow them to develop and dispense those gifts. We are a training center. We must motivate and encourage people to discover and use their spiritual gifts.

a.   *Testing spiritual gifts*

b.   *Training methods for laypeople: night schools, Saturday schools*

C. Ministry Focus of _____

1.   The Ephesians 4:12 passage clearly states that the saints should do, not just know, the ministry. We must encourage all people to share their ministry in the Body and in their secular lives.

2.   The eldership, a pastoral ministry, must encourage people as they develop their ministry gifts.

Modeling..............I do it.

Mentoring...........I do it, and they are with me.

Monitoring..........They do it, and I am with them.

Multiplying.........They do it, and I am in the background.

Equipped............They do it!

Action Ideas

IV. QUESTIONS TO PONDER (from John Maxwell)

A. How Much Time Do I Spend Weekly Equipping Others?

B. How Many Do I Equip?

C. For What Areas Do I Equip them?

D. Am I Committed to an Equipping Ministry?

E. Am I Effective in the Areas I Need to Equip?

F. Am I Willing to Invest My Life in Other People?

G. Am I Willing to Share the Credit?

H. Have I Developed a Prospect List?

I. Do I Have an Equipping Strategy?

Action Ideas

DISCIPLESHIP

SHEPHERDING	EQUIPPING	DEVELOPING
1. Care	1. Training for Ministry	1. Training for Personal Growth
2. Immediate Need Focus	2. Task Focus	2. Person Focus
3. Relational	3. Transactional	3. Transformational
4. Service	4. Management	4. Leadership
5. Ministry	5. Ministry by Addition	5. Ministry by Multiplication
6. Immediate	6. Short Term	6. Long Term
7. Feel Better	7. Unleashing	7. Empowering
8. Available	8. Teaching	8. Mentoring
9. Focus on Nature	9. Focus on Specific Ministry	9. Focus on Specific Leader
10. No Curriculum	10. Curriculum Set	10. Curriculum Flexible
11. Need Oriented	11. Skill Oriented	11. Character, Mind/Heart
12. What do they want?	12. What do I need?	12. What do they need?
13. Masses	13. Many	13. Few
14. Maintenance	14. Science	14. Art

Diagram © John Maxwell

The Lay Pastor and Raising New Leaders

The Lay Pastor & Raising New Leaders

The church today needs qualified leadership for the harvest. Where does a pastor find such leaders? What criteria should be used? If the pastor chooses to train his own leaders, what methods should be used? What specific qualifications should leaders possess?

The Bible is the source book for all pastors endeavoring to build a healthy local church. The process of raising up local leaders must be based on biblical principles. In this study we will cover the following areas:

> *Philippians 2:20 For I have no man like-minded*
>
> *. . . or equal soul*
>
> *. . . as interested as I am*
>
> *. . . for I have no one else as near of my own attitude*
>
> *. . . for I have no one else of kindred spirit*
>
> *. . . no one like disposed*

I. GATHERING POTENTIAL LEADERS: THE NECESSARY RISK

A. The Risk of Gathering _____ Leaders

> *Acts 28:3; Isaiah 11:1-3*

B. The Risk of Gathering _____ Leaders

> *Matthew 8:18-27; John 6:1-20; Leviticus 1:7-17;*
> *Matthew 3:11-12; I Corinthians 3:13; I Peter 1:7;*
> *Revelation 3:18*

C. The Risk of Gathering _____ Leaders

> *James 1:8*

D. The Risk of Gathering _____ Leaders

E. The Risk of Gathering _____ Leaders

F. The Risk of Gathering _____ Leaders

II. BIRTHING KINDRED LEADERS

Genesis 14:13; Psalm 87:1-7

A. Birthed Into the Main Elements of the Local Church

    1. The _____of the house

        Proverbs 29:18

    2. The _____ of the house

        II Chronicles 4:20; I Chronicles 15:13

    3. The _____ of the house

    4. The _____ of the house

    5. The _____ of the house

    6. The _____ of the house

    7. The _____ of the house

B. The Birthing Process

    1. Spiritual _____ with the local church

    2. Spiritual _____ of the inner man

    3. Spiritual _____ of the truths taught

    4. Spiritual _____ to others

    5. Spiritual _____ that is proven in the storm

    6. Spiritual _____ evidenced in faithfulness

Action Ideas

III.   IDENTIFYING POTENTIAL KINDRED LEADERS

A. Why People Volunteer

1.   They want to be needed.

2.   They want to help others. (They like knowing something others do not know.)

3.   They want a sense of belonging and acceptance.

4.   They want self-esteem and affirmation.

5.   They want recognition (lay minister of the week, personal note from the pastor).

6.   They want to be a part of something exciting.

7.   They want to exercise their spiritual gifts.

8.   They are challenged by someone they greatly admire.

B. Why People Do Not Volunteer

1.   They are not asked.

2.   They feel unqualified.

3.   They have no mentors or instructors.

C. Positive Identification Marks

1.   _____

2.   _____

3.   _____

4.   _____

5.   _____

6.   _____

7. _____

8. _____

9. _____

D. Negative Identification Marks

1. _____

2. _____

3. _____

4. _____

5. _____

6. _____

7. _____

8. _____

9. _____

IV. GATHERING POTENTIAL LEADERS: THE DIFFERENT BACKGROUNDS

A. Team Leadership

Often, team leaders are people who have helped the pastor establish a local church. Nevertheless, they too must be birthed into the pastor's ministry. Generally, these people are stable and loyal, with specific gifts and abilities.

B. Inherited Leadership

The new pastor inherits the leadership already in place in an existing church. Sometimes these people are well qualified, good leaders. Sometimes these people have problems and needs. Inherited leaders are accustomed to a certain way of doing tasks and have formed their own concept of the local church.

C. Transplanted Leadership

A transplanted leader may come from many different situations: a Bible college, a denominational church, a restoration-type church, a family, etc. In medicine, a doctor takes great precaution and care in transplanting a heart, liver, kidney, or any vital organ, to prevent the body from rejecting the new organ, and even after such precaution, the body may still turn on the foreign part and destroy the proper function of the whole body.

D. Traditional Leadership

Many times, the pastor initially feels safe in training or using this type of leadership. The traditional leaders may have excellent character qualities, be sincere and eager to work with the pastor. Problems can arise, however, if the pastor is not familiar with their root ideas, concepts, vision, etc. If these people are utilized prematurely, the pastor will have great difficulty in protecting the local body.

E. Novice Leadership

These new leaders may seem well-equipped in fundamental knowledge and necessary character. However, a pastor may act too hastily or lack wisdom and may use them too soon. Under the pressure and demands of ministry, many novice leaders have been destroyed.

F. Home Grown Leadership

LAY PASTOR

Training Manual

The Lay Pastor and Vision for Biblical Product

Action Ideas

The Lay Pastor & Vision for Biblical Product

At one time, craftsmanship was esteemed highly. Gifted craftsmen expended great time, energy, and creativity, producing items which are of great value even today. By the early 1900's, however, assembly-line production took over. Products which had once taken days, weeks, or months to produce could now be manufactured in hours. While the quantity greatly increased, unfortunately, the quality decreased.

This same pattern is reflected in the church today. Many church leaders have tried to mass-produce believers. While they can claim hundreds or thousands in church attendance, often the quality of the "end product" has diminished. As Juan Carlos Ortiz once stated, "Our problem is the eternal childhood of the believer."

But God is interested in the end product (Colossians 1:28-29), and that end product should be a biblical product. We must ask, "What should the end product resemble?" and "Has God given us a biblical pattern to follow?" The crisis in the Church today is that the kind of people being produced are inferior to God's standards.

I.   DEFINING BIBLICAL PRODUCT

A. Biblical Product in Creation

   Genesis 1:26-28

1.   Man was created in God's image, to bear His character.

2.   The purpose was so man could take dominion.

B. Biblical Product in the Old Covenant

1.   God's standard of godly character: obedience to God's authority

2.   God's desire for a people of prayer and worship

3.   God's desire for a people who understood His purpose

   God is willing to use any means necessary to produce a biblical product acceptable to Him.

C. Biblical Product in the New Covenant/Gospels

1. _____.

   Matthew 28:18-20

2. _____.

   Luke 9:23-25

3. _____.

   Luke 14:25-35

4. _____.

   John 8:31

5. _____.

   Matthew 9:36-38

6. _____.

   John 13:34-35

7. _____.

   John 15:7-17

D. Biblical Product as Seen in Acts.

   Acts 2:37-42; 6:7; 9:26; 14:21-24

1. _____

2. _____

E. Biblical Product as Seen in the Epistles

   Colossians 1:26-29; Ephesians 4:12-16; Romans 8:29

1. _____

2. _____

Action Ideas

F. Biblical Product Stated

1. People who are disciples of Christ and in submission to Jesus as Lord

    Luke 14:25-35; 9:23-25

2. People who are filled with and living by the Holy Spirit

    Ephesians 5:17-18

3. People who are functioning in their spiritual gifts

    Romans 12:1-6

4. People who are committed to and supporting the local church

    Acts 2:37-47

5. People who are fervent worshippers

    Colossians 3:16; Ephesians 5:17-18

6. People who are faithful prayers

    Luke 16:1-10

7. People who are bold sharers of their faith

8. People who are generous givers

    II Corinthians 8-9

9. People who are family builders

10. People who are servants to others

11. People who are overcoming the self-life

12. People who have a world vision

G. A.W. Tozer's Seven Marks of a Mature Christian

1. A desire to be holy rather than happy

2. A desire to see the honor of God advanced, even if that means personally suffering temporary dishonor or loss

    3.   A desire to carry one's own cross

    4.   A desire to see everything from God's viewpoint

    5.   A desire to die rather than to live in a wrong manner

    6.   A desire to see others advance at our expense

    7.   Habitually making eternity-conscious judgments rather than temporal judgments

II.   THE PROCESS IN PRODUCING BIBLICAL PRODUCT

    A. The Pattern of Christ

        1.   Disciple–making was Christ's approach to a biblical product.

            a.   *Jesus made himself available to the multitude, but He gave himself to His disciples.*

                Matthew 28:18-20

            b.   *"Disciple" always implies the existence of a personal attachment which shapes the whole life of the disciple; a follower, a student, a disciplined one.*

        2.   Discipleship is a matter of personal involvement.

            Mark 3:13-15; Matthew 9:35-10:5; Luke 6:12; II Timothy 2:2

            a.   *It involves _____.*

            b.   *It involves _____.*

            c.   *It involves _____.*

            d.   *It involves _____.*

            e.   *It involves _____.*

            f.   *It involves _____.*

                II Timothy 2:2

            g.   *It involves _____.*

Action Ideas

> *"It is change, not time, that turns fools into wise men and students into saints."*
>   A.W. Tozer

B. The Pattern of the Apostle Paul

1. Paul established local churches.

    Acts

2. Paul established local leadership.

    Ephesians 4:12-16

3. Paul established a product goal.

    Colossians 1:26-28

4. Paul established a process that involved teaching the Word of God, prayer, authority, submission, and character development.

C. Practical Suggestions for Processing Toward Biblical Product

1. Do not allow quantity to distort the need for quality.

2. Allow the Word of God to set the standard for biblical product, not other churches, trends in culture, or accommodating programs.

3. Process toward biblical product by focusing on people individually through small groups, hands-on counseling, or discipleship groups.

4. Proclaim the New Testament message of Christ's Lordship.

5. Stay sensitive to the ministry of the Holy Spirit in building the church.

6. Establish people in the Word of God through a disciplined teaching ministry (including theology, ecclesiology, pneumatology, history, and eschatology).

7. Involve the entire church in ministries. Establish a variety of teams to utilize their gifts and callings to meet the practical needs of the church and community.

Action Ideas

8. Hold up the historic standard God has given, but also be able to minister to the exception with grace.

9. Provide for the ongoing care of new converts with a view to making them ministers.

The Lay Pastor and Handling Conflict

The Lay Pastor & Handling Conflict

From the very beginning, the Church has experienced ongoing conflict. All churches in every part of the world struggle with the devastating effects of disagreement, discord, and conflict. The Church in the New Testament encountered such problems and survived. In this section, we will explore the sources and causes of conflict, and the correct response to that conflict. From time to time lay pastors will face challenges from people and situations which must be resolved with great wisdom.

I.   DEFINING THE WORD "CONFLICT"

- Webster's Dictionary: From the Latin word *conflictus* which means a striking together, a contest; originally meant to fight, contend, to clash; incompatible; to be in opposition; sharp disagreement; emotional disturbance resulting from a clash.

- Greek Word (*Agon*): A place where the Greeks assembled for the Olympic Pythian games and watched the contest fight of the athletes. This word came to mean struggle or combat.

- *Agon* Translated

    1.   Conflict (*Philippians 1:30; Colossians 2:2*)

    2.   Contention (*I Thessalonians 2:2*)

    3.   Fight (*I Timothy 6:12; II Timothy 4:7*)

    4.   Race (*Hebrews 12:1*)

    5.   Agony (*Luke 22:44*)

II.   BIBLICAL SYNONYMS OF CONFLICT

A. Contention

   Acts 15:39; Proverbs 18:18; I Corinthians 1:11; Proverbs 26:1; 13:10

Action Ideas

1.   Greek word *(eris)*: "To quarrel," especially rivalry or wrangling as in the church at Corinth.

2.   Greek word *(paraoxusmos)*: "To have sharp feelings or emotions toward someone, the effect of irritation."

3.   Greek word *(philoneikia)*: "To be a lover of strife; signifies the eagerness to contend."

B. Strife

1.   Greek word *(erithea)*: "Denotes the wrong ambition, self-seeking rivalry, self-will as being the underlying meaning of the word; hence it denotes party-making; originally meant a day laborer, a worker for wages with no motive to service."

2.   This Greek word is translated seven times in the New Testament.

   a.   *Contentious (Romans 2:8)*

   b.   *Strife in church problems (II Corinthians 12:20)*

   c.   *Strife as a work of the flesh (Galatians 5:20)*

   d.   *Contention as a wrong motive for preaching (Philippians 1:16)*

   e.   *Strife is a result of wisdom which is not from above (James 3:14)*

   f.   *Strife is a wrong spirit in which we live (Philippians 2:3)*

   g.   *Strife (James 3:16)*

C. Discord

   Proverbs 6:16-19

   Greek: "To be in strife; a quarrel or contention."

Action Ideas

III.   SOURCES OF CONFLICT

A. Conflict Is Caused

1.   *When there is inconsistency in practicing clearly established biblical principles.*

2.   *When the leadership violates moral and ethical standards taught to the people.*

3.   *When the leadership presumptuously declares a vision or direction from the Lord and then abruptly abandons or changes from that direction.*

4.   *When the leadership avoids, procrastinates, or ignores the necessity of confronting and handling the problem of those who are sowing seeds of contention.*

5.   *When the leadership causes great confusion by choosing unqualified leaders to serve the people, thereby violating clearly enunciated standards and wisdom.*

6.   *When the leadership carelessly handles an explosive situation without considering the ramifications or makes a hasty decision without prayer.*

7.   *When the leadership does not consistently practice principles of forgiveness (taught in Matthew 18) and thus allows offenses to grow in the church and in the leaders.*

8.   *When the leadership acts independently, violating the spirit of team ministry.*

IV.   HANDLING CONFLICTS CORRECTLY

A. Principles From the Conflict of Acts 15

    1.   The principle of _____ with an honest heart and a teachable spirit

        Acts 15:1-4,6

    2.   The principle of _____ to consider the matter before they speak to the congregation

        Acts 15:6

    3.   The principle of _____

        _____

B. Practical Principles in Handling Conflicts

    1.   The principle of _____

    2.   The principle of _____

    3.   The principle of _____

    4.   The principle of _____

    5.   The principle of _____

    6.   The principle of _____

    7.   The principle of _____

    8.   The principle of _____

    9.   The principle of _____

    10. The principle of _____

V.   AVOIDING CONFLICTS IN THE LEADERSHIP

A. The Last Supper

B. The Acts of Jesus at the Supper

    1.   Laid aside his garments—_____—did not have internal insecurity

    2.   Girded himself with a towel—_____—quality of an unfettered servant

    3.   Washed their feet—humility—_____—seeketh not its own

C. The Significance of His Acts

    1.   _____.

    2.   _____.

    3.   _____.

    4.   _____.

D. Washing One Another

Washing: "Cleansing of leadership through godly confrontation; serving one another with love and sincerity, protecting one another through godly wisdom."

    1.   We are responsible to _____.

    2.   We are responsible to _____.

    3.   We are responsible to _____.

    4.   We are responsible to _____.

E. Conflicts That Must Be Washed

1. Bruising one another with our tongues, passing on evil reports and half truths.

2. Holding and hiding resentments that come from offenses.

3. Having blind spots in our lives that cause us to stumble.

4. Permitting ongoing problems in relationships with other team members due to unresolved past failures and misunderstandings.

5. Making hasty and uninformed judgments against another leader's decisions or procedures.

Action Ideas

Hot Potato 101

A Primer for Church Conflicts

Perhaps it is time for our colleges to introduce a new course in the required curriculum: "Hot Potato 101." Conflicts in the church appear to be inevitable. They must be approached with both firmness and deep sensitivity.

Frequently, problems are camouflaged. The real difficulty is clouded by anger which arises within the heart of the partisans. Until this is dealt with we will never be able to touch the core of the matter and bring lasting resolution.

Human anger is referred to in James 1:20, "The wrath of man worketh not the righteousness of God." A very literal translation reads, "An angry man doesn't do what is right before God" (Beck).

An angry person will not accept responsibility for his own actions. He will transfer his feelings upon another, making it appear someone else has the embittered attitude or is guilty of wrong. A riled person misconstrues facts. Much like a drunken person who loses depth perception, the irate individual sees things out of focus. Thus it is quite clear that until the resentment subsides, the original problem cannot be tackled.

Heated spirits must be cooled down. This begins when a person acknowledges his behavior is reactionary and is willing in some degree to deal with his own inflamed feelings.

As one who has the responsibility of bringing order and healing to traumatized congregations, I have learned to apply these basic principles. Perhaps these can be amplified in that basic course dealing with conflict resolution.

Action Ideas

Facts and Perception of Facts

In these, there may be a vast difference. On one occasion during a church hassle several years ago, a lady said to me, "My husband gets into trouble because he tells it like it is."

I responded, "Your husband may not be telling it like it is; he tells it as he perceives it to be." He might have been correct, yet he might have been somewhat in error.

Three persons can stand on three street corners of the same intersection and observe the same automobile accident. When they make their report and stand witness in court, it may appear to be three different accidents. As far as each witness is concerned, he is presenting "facts" honestly. It is all a matter of perspective and vantage point.

Someone has well said "there are three sides to every story: your side, my side, and the truth." If we can bring people to the place where they will admit there is even a slight possibility they could be wrong, we will tend to take the heat out. And well should we ourselves admit, "I could be in error." The structuring of facts can alter the appearance of the truth. Let us allow margin for error for ourselves and for others.

Provocation and Justification

It is not abnormal to react to what we consider hostile stimuli. How we react can well determine whether we are on the road to peace or war.

We cannot traverse this span of life from the cradle to the coffin without provocation. Some things are bound to antagonize us. The problem surfaces when we respond to the provocation in an un-Christian manner. We tend to justify our reaction on the basis of the nature of the provocation. Let us remember that no provocation ever justifies an un-christ-like response. If our rejoinder is at a carnal level, we are as guilty of offense as is the provocateur.

Action Ideas

When was the Christian call canceled for the turned cheek, the second mile, the cloak and the coat, the loving for hating, the blessing for cursing, and the praying for the spite-filled antagonizers? In more instances than not, church feuds could be settled by large applications of humility and forgiveness by all parties involved. With such doses of Christian medicine, the ill patient will soon respond with a declining fever. "Be ye kind one to another, tenderhearted, forgiving one another, even as God for Christ's sake hath forgiven you" (Ephesians 4:32).

Method and Motive

The apostle Paul speaks strongly on this subject in Philippians 2:3: "Let nothing be done through strife or vainglory; but in lowliness of mind let each esteem others better than themselves." Strife is the wrong method, and vainglory is the wrong motive.

Constant agitation within the church involving matters of little consequence must be viewed as seditious. Generally this is amply mixed with egocentric demonstration. The antidote is humility of mind and Christian deference to our brothers and sisters.

Paul the apostle pegs it well in II Timothy 2:24-26: "And the Lord's servant must not quarrel; instead, he must be kind to everyone, able to teach, not resentful. Those who oppose him he must gently instruct, in the hope that God will grant them repentance leading them to a knowledge of the truth, and that they will come to their senses and escape from the trap of the devil, who has taken them captive to do his will" (NIV).

These, among other considerations, appear to be essential in resolving church conflict. If partisans demonstrate willingness to submit to biblical principles and are sincere in their efforts to see restoration of harmony, then we are well on our way. It is when we subject church tensions to the demands of the "irresistible force" contending with the "immovable object" that wreckage and devastation come. That is an awfully high price to pay. We can't afford to insist on having our own way. Let us rather abide in Christ's beatitude, "Blessed are the peacemakers: For they shall be called the children of God" (Matthew 5:9).

Almon M. Bartholomew, superintendent in New York District for
Advance magazine, November 1983

LAY PASTOR
Training Manual

The Lay Pastor and Counseling

The Lay Pastor & Counseling

Isaiah 9:6-7; Psalm 1; 33:10-11; Colossians 1:9-14; 3:16

I.　INTRODUCTION

- We need to recognize the limitations of one hour. For that reason, I want to recommend the works of Dr. Jay Adams: Competent to Counsel, Shepherding God's Flock, and The Christian Counselor's Manual.

- I must recognize my own limitations in this part of pastoral ministry.

- Our Lord is a wonderful counselor.

    Isaiah 9:6

- A major duty of a shepherd is to provide counsel and guidance.

II.　DEFINING TERMS

- Council (*Sumboulion*) (Greek): "An assembly for consultation; a plurality of presumed qualified persons."

    1.　*Sun*—together

    2.　*Bouleou*—to advise; a gathering to advise

    3.　Also *sunedrion*, from which we get "sanhedrin." *Sunedrion* comes from two Greek words *sun* (together) and *hedrion* (steadfast).

- Counsel: "Advice or corporate wisdom." By definition, it is presupposed that counsel comes out of council, or out of more than one qualified person.

- Counselor: "An advisor." In today's society, the advisor is often a professional person speaking out of secular wisdom, training, and technique.

Action Ideas

- Elements in Counseling

    1. A case history

    2. Personal interviews

    3. Applications of a particular method

    4. Interviews which result in certain conclusions, either explicit or implied

    5. Conclusions that the recipient is left to apply. (In professional counseling there is usually little or no corporeity or ongoing involvement in applying the counsel.)

III.   PRESUPPOSITIONS OF PREVAILING METHODS

(All of these are secular in value and purport to be scientific in method. There are varying views on whether psychology is a science.)

A. Rogerian (Carl Rogers)

1. This method is primarily to mirror the patient's thoughts.

2. It presupposes that man has within himself all the resources he needs. All the counselor has to do is help him to see his problem and unlock his potential.

3. Rogerian counseling usually avoids direct advice or guidance.

B. Freudian (Sigmund Freud)

1. This method is primarily analytical or digging into the person's soul.

2. It presupposes that any man or woman who is not well-adjusted has been wrongly socialized by someone else (i.e., relatives). In developing a super-ego (or an over-arching value structure), he or she has come into conflict with the id (primitive desires). Analysis seeks to uncover the source of the conflict and water down the super-ego, thus removing a sense of guilt. (The conflict is between the super-ego, or cultural morals, and the id, which is the primitive desires.) Most Freudian psychologists see guilt as an artificial and harmful attitude caused by society.

C. Skinnerian (B.F. Skinner)

1. *This method is directed toward behavior modification.*

2. *It presupposes that man is an animal and, like all animals, can be behaviorally controlled scientifically through the control of his environment or biology.*

IV.   PRESUPPOSITIONS OF BIBLICAL COUNSEL

- There is a sovereign God whose will represents man's highest good and greatest joy.

- Jesus Christ is God incarnate and the ultimate revelation of the wisdom of God.

- God is continuously involved in creation through the presence of the Holy Spirit.

- The Holy Scripture is inspired by God and is profitable for instruction, reproof, and rebuke.

    II Timothy 3:16

- Man fell from innocence through disobedience and is inclined to disobedience which causes guilt.

- Man is accountable to God, the Creator and owner of creation.

- Sin is against God and must be atoned for in order to restore man to righteousness, peace, and joy.

- By repentance and faith, man can be restored to God through Jesus Christ's death, burial, and resurrection.

- Through the lordship of Jesus Christ and the work of the Holy Spirit, individuals can live in the will of God and have harmony within themselves.

- Fellowship with the Church strengthens our ability to overcome problems.

Action Ideas

V. ADVICE ON GIVING ADVICE

- _____.

   (Do not be a busybody.) Be sure it is within your God-given sphere. If it is, approach the problem with the spiritual authority God has given to you; He will help you. Expect an answer and expect His power.

- _____

   _____.

   Pastors need biblical knowledge, experience, and maturity. If you have no experience in the particular area you are confronting, consult with your pastor or qualified minister experienced in that area of life. Defer to his expertise, but stay involved with the counselee. You still have pastoral responsibility. Referral does not alleviate that responsibility.

- _____.

   Take notes. Get thoroughly acquainted with the person and the issues. Consider all of the factors such as medical, economical, relational, etc. Consider what measures the person has already taken. Do not omit the spiritual factors.

- _____.

   "To him that answers a matter before he hears it, it is a folly and a shame" (Proverbs 18:13).

- _____.

   Examine them clearly. If need be, write down the choices and reasons, pros and cons, for each. Pray over them.

- _____. Remember . . .

   1. You are an advisor; you are not God.

   2. You could be accountable for the results.

   3. You will continue to be involved with the person after he or she takes your advice.

   4. A right posture in counseling will preserve the integrity of the person you are counseling and allow his or her initiative and convictions to work.

       Make your words sweet and tender. They taste better if you have to eat them later.

Action Ideas

- _____ to give both you and the one you are counseling an answer. He may speak to either of you, and both of you should be able to confirm or give amen. Remember, counseling is from one recipient of God's grace to another. If sin is involved, encourage the person to seek the Lord for a sense of godly sorrow which will motivate him or her to turn from the sin involved, confess it, make right any injuries to others and walk in faith and obedience to the Lord. Do not try to accomplish a change of behavior without repentance and faith.

- In a relational context, _____

  _____.

  The process should go something like this: old patterns > dehabilitation > rehabilitation > new patterns.

- _____.

  Discussion with wife, children, and friends can prove an embarrassing breach of trust, destroy your credibility as a counselor, and bring damage to the person you are counseling.

- _____

  _____.

  1. Always conduct counseling with women in a setting where a secretary or wife is near. If possible, assign that activity to an older and experienced woman.

  2. Avoid an ongoing number of lengthy sessions.

  3. Watch for any changes in your attitude, or hers, which produce an upgrading of appearance or manifestation of affection.

  4. If you sense a problem developing, get to your pastor immediately.

Action Ideas

21 Ways To Get Greater Counseling Results In Less Time

WHEN A PERSON COMES TO YOU WITH A PROBLEM:

- Establish who his "spiritual covering" is (I Corinthians 11:3). Who did God place over their lives? Does a son or daughter have a father and/or mother? Does a woman have a husband? Is the grandfather living? Are they in a Bible-believing local church?

- Discern any evidence of rebellion in him (I Samuel 15:23). Are they under their God-given authorities? Any rebellion exposes them to the realm and power of Satan's control and makes any counseling ineffective until this is corrected.

- Direct him back to his God-given authorities (I Corinthians 14:35; Galations 4:2; etc.). The most effective counseling usually involves exhorting people to get God's direction through His ordained channels. To bypass these authorities is to encourage disloyalty to them and promote reaction by them. Satan usually tries to cut off communication with the one through whom God wants to work.

- Offer to assist his authorities to help him (Matthew 23:11; Philemon). Their authorities will be more ready to trust you when you prove your loyalty to them. Offer to serve them by helping the one who is under their authority at their request.

- Assume that the one who comes with the problem is usually the key to the solution (Romans 2:1-3; Luke 12:13-15; I Corinthians 6:1-10). God often brings pressures into our lives in order to build the character of Christ in us or in others around us. When we react to these pressures, we compound the lack of godliness with judging, disloyalty, lack of love, impatience, covetousness, and resentment.

- Avoid counseling when a person is emotional (Proverbs 25:20). There are times to counsel and there are times to listen and to comfort.

- Ask for a sentence summary of the problem (Proverbs 18:17; 21:2). By asking for a brief written or oral summary of the problem before discussing it, you avoid a common pitfall: listening to many details which are designed to get your sympathy and win your approval of wrong actions or attitudes. Remember that people usually rationalize their sins away.

Action Ideas

- Set up appointments rather than giving immediate counsel (Proverbs 20:5). When you allow a person with a surface problem more time to think about his problem, it often goes away or diminishes in importance. This occurs because the person's emotions change or the situation changes, or more facts are understood. Sometimes a second appointment is effective in concluding the discussion.

- See conflicts as the result of a person resisting God's grace (Titus 2:11-12; James 4:7). When temptations and trials come, God gives the desire and power to respond to them according to His will. When we resist His grace, we experience the "reproofs of instruction."

- Look for evidence of three root problems (Hebrews 12:15-17). The three root problems are bitterness, greed, and moral impurity. Only as you identify and remove these will there be lasting solutions. Check the spirit of the person more than the facts that you are given. Do not assume that a person is a Christian.

- Bind Satan before trying to spoil his house (Mark 3:27). Only when Satan is bound by praying in the name and through the blood of the Lord Jesus Christ will we be able to reclaim the ground he has gained in the life of another. Satan must not be able to find any fault in the one who binds him.

- Expect two levels of problems: surface and root (Proverbs 13:18). A person will often come to you with two problems: One that is "respectable" and then the real problem. That person will see how you accept him and respond to the first problem before trusting you with the second problem. Make sure that you are dealing with the real problem. It is wise to ask: "In addition to that, is there any other problem?" Then wait and listen.

- Learn to be an "instructive listener" (Luke 2:46-47). The person who comes to you for an answer also wants your acceptance. You communicate acceptance by smiling and nodding. The smile signals acceptance of the person; the nod signals acceptance of his ideas. When you cannot accept the person's ideas, stop nodding. Never shake your head to signal "no."

- Stop any discussion of sensual details (Ephesians 5:12; Jude 1:23). Sometimes a person will enjoy telling you shameful details of past sins. That person wants acceptance from you as a representative of God. If you listen to sensual details, you will be ensnared by them. It requires a spiritually mature person to help a brother who is overtaken by a fault—one who will consider himself, lest he also be tempted (Galatians 6:1).

Action Ideas

- Find the point of greatest resistance, and design a project to deal with it (Mark 10:21-22). Lasting help will never come until the person who comes for help is willing to deal with hidden desires and motives. Often the key to the solution has already been rejected and, as a result, the person is ever learning and never able to come to the knowledge of the truth.

- Remember that a persistent habit usually indicates a deeper sin or desire (Psalm 66:18; James 1:14). Satan is only able to conquer us when we regard iniquity in our hearts. We are tempted when we are drawn away by our own lusts. Any secret provision for the flesh will result in defeat in other areas. Sometimes a person is unaware of hidden motives which God is judging in them.

- Never take up offenses for a person (Psalm 15:3). When a person tells you his problems, it is difficult for him not to involve others who hurt him or caused the problem. You must never form opinions of these others or make statements of condemnation about them.

- Help a person see the problem from God's perspective (Romans 8:28-29; II Corinthians 1:4-6). All things work together for good if we love God and are following His calling because it causes us to become more like the Lord Jesus Christ. Most people translate problems according to their own structure of thinking. We need to view them from God's perspective. It is also essential to see that life is designed as a cause and effect sequence. This is explained in Galatians 6:7-8.

- Turn direct statements into questions (Proverbs 15:1). Rather than telling a woman that she has a strong will, ask: "Would you or your husband say that you have a strong will?" If you must make a direct statement of blame, it must be lovingly expressed with a smile. The stronger the statements you make, the longer you must listen first.

- Watch for wrong emotional attachments to you (Jeremiah 17:9). It is very easy for a woman to develop a "love" for the pastor who counsels her. It is for this reason that every wise pastor will teach his men how to be spiritual leaders, to know how to bind Satan and to build a spiritual hedge of protection around their own families.

- Help each person turn past problems into a significant life message (Psalms; Isaiah 61:1-3). God gives beauty for ashes when we are able to share with others in a discreet way how we applied basic scriptural principles to gain more of the character of Christ. This turns the guilt of the past into a motivating reminder that we belong to God because we have been redeemed by His blood.

Resource material from 1979 Institute in Basic Youth Conflicts.

The Lay Pastor and the Web Principle

The Lay Pastor & the Web Principle

I. THE WEB PRINCIPLE OF GROWTH

A. Reason for Initial Attendance in Church

1. Evangelistic crusade............................0.3%

2. Transfer within city 5.6%

3. Pastor..6.5%

4. Relatives...14.8%

5. Friends...48.2%

6. Transferred from out of town.............12.6%

7. Walked in 4.8%

8. Other..7.2%

B. *Oikos* Evangelism

Oikos is the Greek word for household. It refers to a strategy of identifying existing "webs" of friends and relatives as the prime source of prospects for church growth.

1. Luke 8:39

2. Luke 19:9

3. John 4:53

4. Acts 10:2

5. Acts 18:8

6. I Corinthians 1:16

7. Mark 2:14-15

8.   Luke 7:37 - 8:3

9.   John 1:40-45

C. Importance of the Web Principle Today

Webs of common kinship (the larger family), common community (friends and neighbors), and common interests (associates, work relationships, recreation) are still the paths most people follow in becoming Christians today. Here are some simple, yet profound, reasons why "*oikos* evangelism" should be a major part in the outreach of any church.

1.   It is the natural way small groups and churches grow.

2.   It is the most cost-effective way to reach new people.

3.   It is the most fruitful way to win new people.

4.   It provides a constantly enlarging source of contacts.

5.   It brings the greatest satisfaction to members.

6.   It results in the most effective assimilation of new members.

7.   It tends to win entire families.

8.   It uses existing relationships.

II.   HOW THE WEB PRINCIPLE WORKS

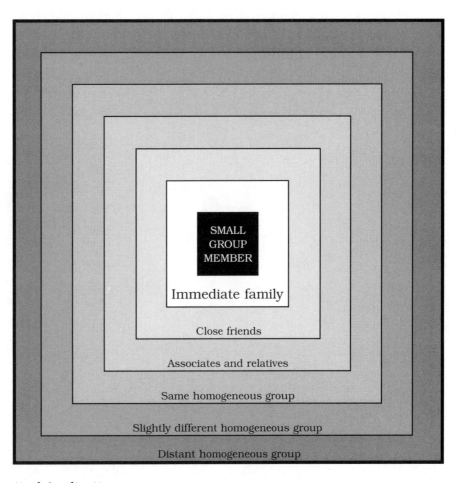

- Practical Application

    1.   List three families that are unsaved and not going to church.

    2.   Small group leader checks with people of the small group then goes with the member to visit this family.

    3.   Think up strategies to get new people contacted within your web.

    4.   Pray for the web list.

- Each church member has approximately 8 to 12 unchurched people in his web. A small group of 35 members could have the prospect of nearly 300!

III.   MISSION SEVENTY MEDITATIONS

- **Mission Seventy**: The appointing and sending of ordinary people into ordinary places of society to reap an extraordinary harvest of people for Christ.

    Luke 10:1-29 (especially verse 1-2); Matthew 28:19

    1. _____. Each human life is precious to God, yet every one of these precious people, outside of Christ's salvation, will be eternally lost.

        Romans 3:10-19; 2:14-16; Genesis 2:17; Proverbs 14:12; Luke 13:5; 16:19-31; Revelation 14:10-11

    2. _____. God has not predestined anyone to hell. Eternity is by choice. We all must choose; God has given us Christ.

        Hebrews 7:25; Matthew 8:2-3; I Timothy 2:3-4; II Peter 3:9; Ephesians 1:4

    3. _____

        _____.

        The only way is through believing in Christ, His sinless life, and His atoning death.

        Isaiah 1:6; Matthew 9:12; John 3:36; Ephesians 2:12; II Corinthians 5:19

    4. God has freely given us salvation through His Son and now has

        _____.

        I Peter 3:18; John 10:11; Romans 8:16

    5. _____. We already have the Holy Spirit to enable us to proclaim the gospel message by the power of the Holy Spirit, God working with us with supernatural signs.

        Acts 1:8; 11:24; I Peter 4:10; Ephesians 4:7; I Corinthians 12:7; II Timothy 1:6; I Timothy 4:14

Action Ideas

6. _____

_____. We must communicate the gospel message in a manner maximizing the likelihood of a positive soul-saving response.

7. _____

_____. Christ's second coming will end this time period with the resurrection of the dead; each human being shall be committed to either heaven or hell for eternity.

> *Matthew 13:42; Revelation 2:11; 20:6,15; Daniel 12:2; Matthew 25:46; Jude 1:7*

8. God has warned that every believer will stand before God's throne and be _____

_____

_____.

> *Matthew 25:10,23; 28:19-20*

- Mission Seventy Target People List

    1. This list should be taken from the group. Limit each person or couple to two names (two families or singles).

    2. The names for the list should be collected at this meeting and then kept for each mid-month meeting (or possibly sometimes during your Sunday meeting) to be prayed over specifically.

LAY PASTOR

Training Manual

The Lay Pastor and Closing the Back Door

Action Ideas

The Lay Pastor & Closing the Back Door

Matthew 28:18-29; Colossians 1:28-29; Ephesians 4:11-16; John 17:12

It is clear by the scriptures listed above that Christ is interested in every member of His Body and has commissioned the Church, especially leaders in the Church, to strive toward assimilation of every member the Lord has given to that body. As we pray for the harvest to come from the north, south, east, and west, according to Isaiah 43:5-7, the Lord answers our prayers and brings them in. As with the Lord Jesus, it is our desire that we not lose any that the Lord intends to be part of this Body.

Unfortunately, in all churches, and especially larger ones, it is relatively easy for individuals to slip out the "back door" of the church and drop into inactivity. In this lesson we will attempt to explain why some people leave the church and what we can do to keep the ones God has given us.

I.   WHO ARE THE DROPOUTS?

A. A Complex Question with a Complex Answer

B. A 1978 Gallup Study

C. Misconceived Ideas

1.   They are superficial types of people.

2.   They really were never part of us.

3.   They are not spiritual enough to handle our worship, preaching, commitment, etc.

4.   They have an attitude.

Action Ideas

II. FACTORS INFLUENCING INACTIVITY

    A. Age—Teenagers are the Highest Drop-Out Rate.

    B. Lifestyle Interruptions—They Lose the Habit of Coming Due to Moving, Illness, or Work Schedule Changes.

    C. Marital Satisfaction

    D. Individualism

    E. Anxiety, Anger, Conflict—These Feelings are the Highest Reasons for Dropping Out.

    F. Social Needs/Friendship

    G. Pastoral Ministry

    H. Social Action

III. OUR ATTITUDES TOWARD DROPOUTS

    A. Common Stereotypes and Attitudes

        1. They do not love God.

        2. They do not love church.

        3. The have no real eternal value system.

        4. They probably drop out of everything they start.

    B. The Unconscious Timeline

        "I'll give the church 6-8 weeks to contact me or else I know what I feel about this church is right."

IV. WHAT CAN WE DO?

    A. Make Sure New Members are Properly Assimilated.

        1. The importance of _____

Action Ideas

2. The importance of _____

3. The importance of _____

4. The importance of _____

B. Become Aware of Tell-Tale Signs.

Eight Weigh-Stations on the Way Out:

1. The person verbalizes his/her irritations or difficulties with someone or something.

2. If no one seems to pay attention to what the person says, he/she says it louder.

3. If getting louder does not cause the person to get attention, he/she becomes angry.

4. The person begins to be absent from worship services.

5. The person hopes that someone will take note of the fact that he/she is no longer attending regularly and expects that someone will call or visit him/her to find out why.

6. If no one seeks out the person, he/she ceases to provide financial support to the congregation.

7. The person finds himself/herself feeling very helpless to correct the situation.

8. The person stops caring about the relationship with the congregation.

C. Do not Let that Thought Pass Through Your Mind Without Contacting Someone.

D. Develop Active Listening Skills.

*Resource material from Fuller Seminary "**Closing the Back Door**" Seminar.*

LAY PASTOR

Training Manual

The Lay Pastor and Intercessory Prayer

Action Ideas

The Lay Pastor & Intercessory Prayer

Isaiah 59:16; Jeremiah 27:18; Revelation 5:8; 8:3-4; Exodus 8:28

We venture into new territory as we seek to understand the potent ministry of prayer intercession. This is vital to our future, essential to fulfilling our vision. As a local church called by God to reach our city, our nation, and the nations of the world, intercession is the key requirement. This is a high calling with a price to pay, but the benefits far outweigh the costs. Let us set out together to grasp fully the prayer of intercession, determined to become people zealous to see the fulfillment of God's purposes.

I.   SEVEN BASIC TRUTHS REGARDING INTERCESSION

- Intercessory prayer is found in Scripture from Genesis to Revelation as a definite kind of prayer God responds to.

- Intercessory prayer is modeled by many of God's chosen leaders who practiced the ministry of intercession with awesome results.

- Intercessory prayer was a prayer commitment of the first apostles, the first disciples, the first church.

- . Intercessory prayer was and is the chief ministry of our Lord Jesus Christ, who is the mediator between God and man and is the intercessor for man now.

- Intercessory prayer is the responsibility of every church that is ruled by Christ and His Word.

- Intercessory prayer is being restored to the Church world-wide in what might be the greatest unified emphasis since the first church in the Book of Acts.

- Intercessory prayer is a call of the Spirit to our churches now—today—for the taking of our cities, our regions, and our nations for the Kingdom of God.

Action Ideas

II.   THE FOUR-FOLD CALL TO INTERCESSION FOR THE WHOLE CHURCH

> *I Timothy 2:1; Luke 1:13; 2:37; II Corinthians 1:11;*
> *II Corinthians 9:14*

- Prayers: _____

- Supplications: _____

- Giving of Thanks: _____

- Intercession: _____

III.   THE MEANING OF INTERCESSION

A. Defining Scriptural Words for Intercession

1.   Hebrew

a.   *Palal (84 times): "To pray, to intervene, mediate as a judge, to come between two parties."*

I Samuel 2:25

b.   *Paga (44 times): "To encounter, meet with, reach or stretch unto, to entreat, to strike or touch, to attack."*

2.   Greek

a.   *Entunchano: "To fall in with, meet with in order to converse, to plead with a person with strong feelings."*

Acts 25:24; Romans 11:2; Hebrews 7:25; Romans 8:27,31

b.   *Huperentenchano: "To make a petition or intercede on behalf of another." It is used in Romans 8:26-27 for the work of the Holy Spirit in the believer making intercession.*

c.   *Enteuxis: " A lighting upon, meeting with a person by appoint-ment so as to offer petitions, supplications, and prayers on behalf of another."*

I Timothy 2:1; 4:5

B. Defining the Meaning of Intercession

1.   "An intercessor is a man or woman or child who fights on behalf of others. As such, intercession is the activity that identifies us most with Christ. To be an intercessor is to be like Jesus because that is what Jesus is like. He ever lives to intercede" (Dick Eastman).

2.   "Intercession can be a part of our lives now, the kind of prayer that works the impossible and sets new boundaries of possibility. The spirit of intercession is a bold understanding through prayer of whatever asserts itself against God's design for mankind. Holy Spirit begotten intercessions forecast new life, new hope, and new possibilities for individuals in the impossible" (Jack Hayford).

3.   Intercessory prayer is intensified praying which involves three special ingredients: identification of the intercessor with the one whom is interceded for; agony to feel the burden, the pain, the suffering, the need; authority. This is the gained position of the inter-cessor, to speak with authority that sees results" (*Rees Howells, Intercessor* by Norman Grubb).

4.   "It is apparent that prayer lies close to the gift of the Holy Spirit. New Testament prayer was shown variously to be earnest, even importunate, a matter of steadfastness and devotion, a day-by-day continuing of intercession. The church seen in the Book of Acts was given over to the prayer of intercession with supernatur-al results" (*Renewal Theology*).

5.   "History belongs to the intercessors" (Walter Wink).

6.   "We are working with God to determine the future. Certain things will happen in history if we pray right" (*Celebration of Disciplines* by Richard Foster).

Action Ideas

IV.   THE PRAYER OF INTERCESSION

Isaiah 62:6-7

- To intercede with a _____

     Ruth 1:16; Isaiah 53:6; Genesis 23:8; James 5:15-16; Genesis 32:24-28; Hosea 12:4

- To intercede by _____

     Joshua 8:18

- To intercede by _____

     "Who stood in the way" (Exodus 5:20)

     Romans 8:26-27; Exodus 15:25

- To intercede by _____

     Joshua 19:11,22,26-27,34

- To intercede by _____

     Numbers 35:19; Judges 8:21; I Samuel 22:17-18

- To intercede by _____

     Job 36:32; Isaiah 53:12; 59:16; Exodus 17:12

- To intercede by _____

     Isaiah 23:4; Galatians 4:19; I Thessalonians 2:9; John 16:21; Isaiah 54:1-2; Joel 1:8,5,9-10; Lamentations 2:18-19

For further resource information refer to: **"Gap Standing and Hedge Building"** *tape series—available through BT Publishing.*

The Lay Pastor and Personal Spiritual Warfare

Action Ideas

The Lay Pastor & Personal Spiritual Warfare

Isaiah 42:13; Isaiah 54:17

In spiritual warfare one must never underestimate or overestimate the strength of the enemy. The Lord is with His army and will not fail us. We fight in His name and power, whereas our enemies fight in their own power. We fight with enemies who have been spoiled, whose weapons are blunted, whose power is limited. We know from Scripture that spiritual warfare is a fact. We must fight. We will encounter real satanic opposition. We also know from Scripture that we will win if we follow the biblical guidelines for winning spiritual battles. Satan reigns over an aerial kingdom of hierarchies and spiritual powers and a kingdom on earth in the world. He governs by means of an organized, evil, spiritual network.

I. SPIRITUAL SATANIC NETWORKS WE STRUGGLE AGAINST

- Ephesians 6:10,12-13 "In conclusion, be strong in the Lord—be empowered through your union with Him; draw your strength from Him—that strength which His [boundless] might provides. For we are not wrestling with flesh and blood—contending only with physical opponents—but against the despotisms, against the powers, against [the master spirits who are] the world rulers of this present darkness, against the spirit forces of wickedness in the heavenly (supernatural) sphere. Therefore put on God's complete armor, that you may be able to resist and stand your ground on the evil day [of danger], and having done all [the crisis demands], to stand [firmly in your place]" (Amplified).

- "I need to learn as much as possible about spirit warfare. Our struggle out there is not against the climate, the malaria, or the false religions. Our struggle is against the principalities and powers, against the world rulers of this present darkness, against the spiritual hosts of wickedness in heavenly places" (Bernie May, director of Wycliffe Bible Translators).

- "The early Christians perceived that every nation, tribe and tongue, every people group, was presided over by a spiritual power" (Walter Wink).

SATAN'S NETWORK
II Cor. 4:4; Eph. 2:2; Jn. 12:31; I Jn.5:19

PRINCIPALITIES

LEADERS OF AN ORDER OR RANK

RULERS OF DARKNESS

GOVERNORS IN SEATS OF AUTHORITY

SPIRITUAL POWERS

DEMONIC SPIRITS ATTACKING CONTINUALLY

II. SPIRITUAL WARFARE: SATAN'S STRATEGIES FOR YOUR DEFEAT AND DESTRUCTION

- "Be well-balanced—temperate, sober-minded; be vigilant and cautious at all times. For that enemy of yours, the devil, roams around like a lion roaring in fierce hunger, seeking someone to seize upon and devour. Withstand him. Be firm in faith against his onset, rooted, established, strong, immovable and steadfast" (I Peter 5:8-9)(Amplified).

  "The thief does not come except to steal, and to kill, and to destroy" (John 10:10).

A. Satan's General Strategy

    1. "Stand against the wiles of the devil" (Ephesians 6:11).

        Wiles (methodia) (Greek): "To follow up and investigate by methods and a settled plan, to plan crafty tricks, schemes."

    2. ". . . in order that Satan might not take advantage"
       (II Corinthians 2:11).

        Advantage (pleonekteo) (Greek): "Wanting more, to take the greater part, to plunder."

    3. ". . . for we are not unaware of his schemes" (II Corinthians 2:11).

        Schemes (noema) (Greek): "To have a definite thought against, to ponder at length, to plan very meticulously, to strategize."

B. Satan's Specific Strategy

    1. Quickly _____sown into our hearts through preaching, prayer, and rhema-quickened words before the seed can take root.

        Matthew 13:19

    2. Quietly and persistently _____ and the spiritual ground God has given you, setting up his ownership little by little.

        Ephesians 4:1

    3. Repeatedly _____ to shake our assurance, cripple our confidence, and devastate our future hopes and dreams.

        Revelation 12:9-11

    4. _____ by a chain of unusual bad experiences, irritations, or small calamities so that he may destroy our faith and gain control over us through fear.

        Matthew 17:15; Acts 10:38; II Corinthians 12:7; Isaiah 59:19

    5. _____

       by attacking key leaders or key people, creating a spirit of negativism, magnifying little problems, relational conflicts, producing spiritual unrest, murmuring: any way or anything to cause divi-

Action Ideas

sion that will stop spiritual momentum.

I Samuel 57:14; 62:10

C. Satan's Seasonal Strategy

Luke 4:13

1. Satanic attacks in _____

    Genesis 49:22-26

2. Satanic attacks in _____

    Genesis 15:11; Matthew 18:18-23

3. Satanic attacks in _____

    Exodus 14:15-16; I Corinthians 16:9

4. Satanic attacks in _____

    Daniel 9:3-4; 10:12-14

III. SPIRITUAL WARFARE 101: OUR WEAPONS

A. The Weapon of Spiritual Knowledge and Insights Concerning Satan's Ways

II Corinthians 2:11

B. The Weapon of Spiritual Strength and Security from Christ's Work on the Cross

Revelation 12:11; I John 3:8; Colossians 2:15

C. The Weapon of Spiritual Placement and Commitment to My Church, My Spiritual Family

Ephesians 4:16; Proverbs 27:8; I Corinthians 12:18,28

D. The Weapon of Personal Prayer and Corporate Prayer for Renewing and Refocusing

Ephesians 6:18; Deuteronomy 32:30; Acts 1:14

E. The Weapon of Using God's Word for Defeating the Devil

"You are of God, little children, and have overcome them, because He who is in you is greater than he who is in the world" *(I John 4:4).*

"Yet in all these things we are more than conquerors through Him who loved us" *(Romans 8:37).*

"For though we walk in the flesh, we do not war according to the flesh. For the weapons of our warfare are not carnal but mighty in God for pulling down strongholds" *(II Corinthians 10:3-4).*

"'No weapon formed against you shall prosper, and every tongue which rises against you in judgment you shall condemn. This is the heritage of the servants of the LORD, and their righteousness is from Me,' says the LORD" *(Isaiah 54:1).*

"Yet Michael the archangel, in contending with the devil, when he disputed about the body of Moses, dared not bring against him a reviling accusation, but said, 'The Lord rebuke you!'" *(Jude 1:9).*

"The LORD will cause your enemies who rise against you to be defeated before your face; they shall come out against you one way and flee before you seven ways" *(Deuteronomy 28:7).*

"The angel of the LORD encamps all around those who fear Him, and delivers them" *(Psalm 34:7).*

"And they overcame him by the blood of the Lamb and by the word of their testimony, and they did not love their lives to the death" *(Revelation 12:11).*

"Therefore submit to God. Resist the devil and he will flee from you. Draw near to God and He will draw near to you. Cleanse your hands, you sinners; and purify your hearts, you double-minded" *(James 4:7-8).*

LAY PASTOR

Training Manual

Appendix

Lay Pastor's Job Description

Lay Pastor is the recognizing of the pastoral gift in those who are trained and released to do the work of pastoring while still employed in full-time secular work and not necessarily ordained as an elder (in Bible Temple, the lay pastor has made a 3-5 year commitment and has completed one year of training). We have divided the lay pastors into two different categories: lay pastors over small groups and lay pastors over those people who are not attending small groups.

The Main Responsibilities of a Lay Pastor Over a Small Group Include:

1. Developing and maintaining relationships with each of the small group leaders;

2. Rotating to different small groups to ensure that the entire body receives ministry;

3. Providing counseling support, as needed, for small group leaders;

4. Making sure that baby and wedding showers, hospital visitations and elderly/widow visitations are effectively being handled through each small group.

5. Providing vision, training, and encouragement to evangelize and multiply.

The Main Duties of a Non-Small Group Lay Pastor Include:

1. Calling and inviting those people, who for whatever reason are out of the church's working system, into their homes and connecting them with people and programs for effective assimilation into the church;

2. Touching (i.e., calling, meeting, caring, talking, etc.) these people at least two to four times a year;

3. Providing counseling support as needed for non-small group people.

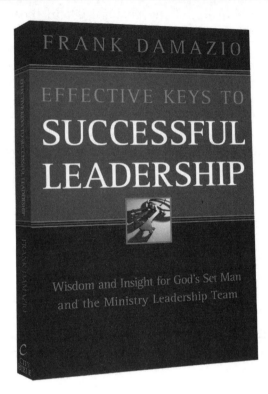

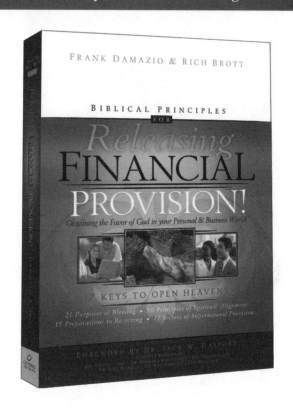

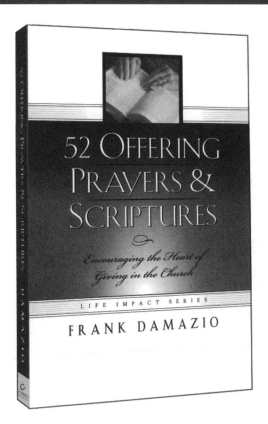

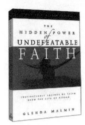

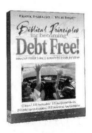

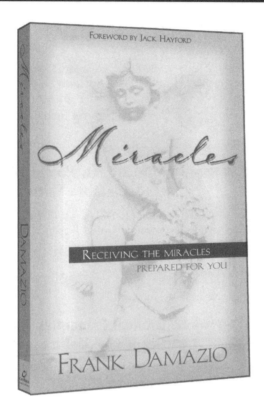

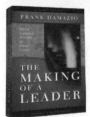
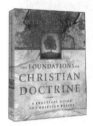

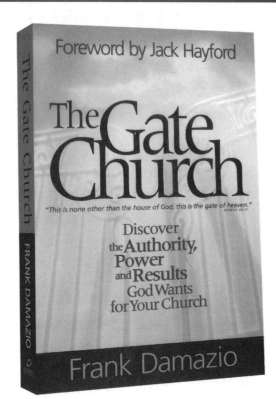